On Revision

Chicago Guides
to *Writing,* Editing*
and Publishing

On Revision

The Only Writing That Counts

WILLIAM GERMANO

THE UNIVERSITY OF CHICAGO PRESS

CHICAGO AND LONDON

The University of Chicago Press, Chicago 60637
The University of Chicago Press, Ltd., London
Published 2021
Printed in the United States of America

30 29 28 27 26 25 24 23 22 21   1 2 3 4 5

ISBN-13: 978-0-226-41051-7 (cloth)
ISBN-13: 978-0-226-41065-4 (paper)
ISBN-13: 978-0-226-41079-1 (e-book)
DOI: https://doi.org/10.7208/chicago/9780226410791.001.0001

Page vii: the Perkins epigraph is quoted in *Editor to Author:
Letters of Maxwell E. Perkins*, ed. John Hall Wheelock
(New York: Scribner's, 1950), 178.

Library of Congress Cataloging-in-Publication Data

Names: Germano, William P., 1950–, author.
Title: On revision : the only writing that counts / William
    Germano.
Other titles: Chicago guides to writing, editing, and publishing.
Description: Chicago : University of Chicago Press, 2021. | Series:
    Chicago guides to writing, editing, and publishing | Includes
    bibliographical references and index.
Identifiers: LCCN 2021010998 | ISBN 9780226410517 (cloth) |
    ISBN 9780226410654 (paperback) | ISBN 9780226410791 (ebook)
Subjects: LCSH: Manuscripts—Editing. | Authorship. | Academic
    writing.
Classification: LCC PN145 .G44 2021 | DDC 808.02—dc23
LC record available at https://lccn.loc.gov/2021010998

♾ This paper meets the requirements of ANSI/NISO Z39.48-1992
(Permanence of Paper).

for our better versions

Teaching is about taking things apart; writing is about putting things together.

TONI MORRISON, INTERVIEWED BY HILTON ALS IN THE *NEW YORKER* (2003)

What's the story, morning glory?

"THE TELEPHONE HOUR," FROM THE MUSICAL *BYE BYE BIRDIE* (1960)
(ALSO THE TITLE OF A 1995 ALBUM BY OASIS)

You must not take what I say as definite at all ever, but all as by way of example only. The whole thing might perhaps be done in some quite different way, and what I say are only suggestions toward the final effect. The ways and means to it may be different from what I have used to illustrate.

EDITOR MAX PERKINS, OFFERING WRITING ADVICE TO MARJORIE KINNAN RAWLINGS (WINNER OF THE 1939 PULITZER PRIZE IN LITERATURE FOR HER NOVEL *THE YEARLING*)

O rocks! Tell us in plain words.

MOLLY BLOOM, WANTING CLARIFICATION, IN *ULYSSES* (1922)

Contents

1

Press start

I'm a terrible birder. Not just inattentive but inept. Binoculars are a birder's tool, but first you need to know what you're looking for.

Sure, egrets and red-tailed hawks are easy to spot, and from an Amtrak car I once saw a bald eagle at the edge of the Hudson. Birds move fast, hide from us, resemble other birds, are residents or visitors. In good weather, and if the whoosh of Manhattan traffic isn't too intrusive, my urban window pipes in morning birdsong from invisible birds. I know they're only sparrows and such, but I enjoy the stupid wonder of knowing they're out there, safe from my prying eyes.

Bird calls are distinctive, so birders assure me, but I haven't put in the time to learn them. In Central Park I can come across real birders, as silent as statues, pointing sturdy field glasses at something—what? somewhere? *where?*—when all I see above me is blue and green and shadow. I have to be content with the very secondhand thrill of being *that* close to a rare migratory species (*there it is*, somebody whispers), a brushstroke making a brief stop in urban greenery as it heads south or north. At least I've learned that I'll hear a bird before I see it—a call or just a few leaves rustling where—what? over there?—disturb the underbrush.

I must have had Anne Lamott's *Bird by Bird: Some Instructions on Writing and Life* in mind when I wrote those paragraphs. Lamott's bestseller takes its title from a family anecdote, her ten-year-old brother freezing up at the prospect of writing a report on birds. Lamott writes that when the boy is "immobilized by the hugeness of the task ahead" his wise parent advises him to take it bird by bird.[1]

Lamott's book is no more about birds than this one is, and she's writing about fiction, not academic prose, but there's a kinship in metaphor. A day at a time, a step at a time, a detail at a time. For academic writers, that might mean another research monograph or article, an archive box, a theory, another endless Google search. Our birds are bigger, more complicated now. And though we might have trained professionally for exactly the kind of writing we've taken on, we can all feel immobilized by the hugeness of the task ahead, at least sometimes.

The world of birds, the world of words. *Listen.* There's so much to read with your ears. And to reread and re-hear. That's what both writing and revising need, and that's what *On Revision* is really about. One version at a time. One revision, then another.

Pick up anything well written and you can learn something about how writing works. Look for and listen to good writing the way you might look for birds, paying attention not just to bright colors and big forms (cardinals, hawks, eagles) but also to sounds, both the calls and the rustling high in the canopy or right there at your feet.

---

1. *Bird by Bird: Some Instructions on Writing and Life* (New York: Anchor, 1995), 18.

Good writing has a convincing shape. But it doesn't just look good on the page. It *sounds* good. You already know that. It's not a secret that successful writers have somehow kept to themselves. You can often hear what makes the writing good even before you're fully conscious of the meaning of a sentence or the import of an argument. That's not a trivial response to writing, either.

So the best rule for revising your writing is the simplest: listen to it. It's the best way to write, too. That took me a long time to figure out. Read it out loud.

But of course when you hear people (including me) say, "Read it out loud," they mean all sorts of things.

Read it out loud, and you'll hear how confusing it is.

Read it out loud, and you'll hear that you repeat the same words again and again.

Read it out loud, and you'll hear that your strongest point flies by too quickly.

Read it out loud, and you'll hear what's happening, moment by moment. You'll hear that puzzling sentence that sets the reader up and then stops short. The spot where your voice changes so much that it's as if somebody else is suddenly talking.

Read it out loud, and you'll find the bit where you sound as if you're getting bored, and then the spot, right there, where your energy and enthusiasm burst from the page.

Can you hear all that?

Writing isn't just well-structured sound, of course. It's sound about something, sound in the service of something. Writing and rewriting and rewriting—the thing and its revision—depend on what we might call *acoustic reading*. Sound plus something. Somehow good writing becomes even better writing when you listen really hard, listen to how the ideas move, pause, and take off again, almost as if they knew more about where to go than you do.

Because they do.

Every writer is Jacob wrestling, not with an angel but with an angle. What's more, each Jacob has to find that angle first. Either at the beginning of a project or belatedly, during a long second (or third) look at what's been drafted, you'll have to discover what you want to say and why you think others will want to hear it. Revising might be the first time you really understand what you've been saying, but it's definitely the last time you can say it before you hand it over to an editor, and from an editor on to the world.

What's true for what you're writing has been true for the book you're reading now. Given its subject, I think I owe you at least a brief account of how *On Revision* came to be. For a long time, I've wanted to think through, on paper, what was important about revising writing, especially revising complex writing. I thought others would want to read about that, too, mainly because revising is a problem every writer faces. And, frankly, I couldn't find anything that had more than a few encouraging pages about how (much less why) to revise academic writing.

Was there a gap in the literature? Or was revision just too difficult to write about? It's one thing to go through a student's paper or offer a sympathetic read of a colleague's working draft, but what exactly—and I want to emphasize that elusive quality of exactness here—could one say about revising writing that a professional writer, or a professional in training, or an advanced student wouldn't already know?

I told myself that writing this book would not be so hard to do. I'd had plenty of what counts as experience. In my first career I had worked as an editor and publisher of scholarly books, tackling the weaknesses and undeveloped potential of very good and sometimes very great manuscripts. Everything you work on as an editor becomes part of your own capacity to read and reread, write and rewrite, and to help others do just that.

I'm a teacher, too. For the last fifteen years I've been working with smart undergraduates at Cooper Union, a small college that specializes in engineering, art, and architecture and where, I remind my students as gently as possible, no one is admitted *because* they're great writers (and, yes, some are). My first-year students and I work together on reading and thinking and writing, and not simply "on writing": that would be meaningless, or at least meaningless to me. Surely my time in the classroom, in tandem with that earlier part of my work life, had given me the keys to writing about revision.

Finally, though probably most important to my sense that a book about revision was possible, I'd written books before. Whatever I had been able to do with and for other writers' projects, I had also done in some way with my own. I'd drafted and discarded, reorganized and reworded, made large-scale changes and fine-tuned, and if I didn't always know exactly why I had done those things with my own words, I had at least built up a body of firsthand experience *as a writer* that I could now go back to and think through. *From Dissertation to Book* was meant to be something like a car repair manual for doctoral students and recent PhDs. The advice it offers still seems good to me, but in what you're reading now I wanted to swim further from shore, not just to think about revising any particular sort of scholarly work but to ask a bigger question: What do we think we're doing when we write and when we rewrite?

Getting *On Revision* down on paper, however, turned out to be a challenge. The pages you're holding have been revised and re-angled many, many times. I drafted a full manuscript, submitted it to Chicago, and studied the reader reports as soon as they arrived. My manuscript needed more work. So I went back and pulled the stitching out, and read and read and reread what I'd drafted, listening for lines that didn't quite do what I needed them to. Was this passage too schematic, that one too anecdotal? It seemed that I had written *a* version of this book, but not *the* version.

I went back to my own premises and my own questions, back to my own *archives* (a concept we'll look at in the pages to follow). I knew I wasn't writing a reviser's style guide. I knew that I wanted to bring into the same frame both a philosophy of writing, especially as it applies to the range of forms and styles that academic publishers engage, as well as some centrally important practical issues. If I were going to revise my own manuscript effectively (insert as much irony here as you like), I would need to keep both in mind. This book, a thing much revised, is both less and more than the version I first crafted. But all of that is irrelevant to you as a reader because what you see now is the only version that I'm showing you. If every worthwhile thing you read by anyone anywhere is merely the last revision in a series of revisions, even if you think of every published text as the final performance after months of rehearsals, elisions, recantations, and sparks of happy insight, and even even if, as you engage whatever you're reading, you crack open your store of readerly sympathy and indulge just the smallest awareness of all the word-churning that's gone into what's on the page, you will reasonably stop yourself and say, "That doesn't matter. I can only read what the writer has put right here." And that's the way it has to be. The writer's lament "But I worked so hard on it!" doesn't cut it. Writers know this simple, hard truth, and that's why they revise, and why they work so hard, even on revising.

But how to think past seemingly aimless word-churning?

Guiding principles can help us, as can targets and a few rules. Plus instinct. Process isn't just mechanics. In Ludwig Bemelmans's classic children's book *Madeline*, the attentive Miss Clavel senses that "something is not right" in the old house in Paris all covered with vines. Has Miss Clavel heard a cry? Or does her instinct tell her something first? (Spoiler alert: Madeline has appendicitis, and it all turns out fine.)

To any writer—you, for instance—instinct is invaluable. You arrive at what we call instinct through practice and the evidence of sensory clues. Instinct feels like something you make, or build, or develop. It would be hard to write or revise without instinct. But what is instinct, anyway? Maybe instinct is the name we give to all the essential writerly skills we can't otherwise identify.

Identifiable skills, practical techniques, working notes, instinct, gut feeling, hunches. Though they may sound like an unlikely troupe of players, when you write and revise you call on all of them. But no tool for working your way into a draft is more important than just reading it as carefully as your ears will let you and staying focused on what you intended to say. *Say*, not just describe or explain, even if your project requires that some things are described and some other things are explained. Revision is less a matter of fixing errors than of saying more clearly, thinking your writing through from the ground up so that you know why you're doing something, why you're going somewhere, why you're taking your reader somewhere with you.

Revising, not as correcting and not as wholesale reinventing. Revision as adjusting: an attentive revision often involves tweaking the course of your thinking or, as the electronic voice says in your car, "Recalculating route." You might think you're lost, at least for a few minutes, until you realize that in revising you've backed away from a path that wouldn't take you anywhere. Recalculate route often enough and you'll think of it as an instinctive ability to learn from being lost, even how to get un-lost. You may learn new routes, too.

Instinct and attention. If writing a good first draft is a kind of informed listening, then a revision of that draft is just more of the same, only with fewer messy bits. When you're done you cross your fingers that the new version works. You'll know by now that this isn't a cookbook, much less a speedy shortcut to writerly nirvana. In fact, the two chapters immediately ahead are meant to slow you down a bit, to get you to reflect on what you have, what you know, what you want to say better. Then come three chapters that focus on three ways to think about your revision. It's not a series of choices; you need all three. Then comes a summing up. The book is short so that you can read it, think about its points, and get back to work on your own writing, even if that means getting lost, and un-lost, and finding a route to better.

Whether *On Revision* does in fact work as I hoped it would is a judgment for others to render, because that's what happens when readers read. I can only claim that I listened as hard as I could to make the best version I was able to make. You're the reader who's a writer. Now it's up to you.

2

Good to better

So you've just finished writing something? Congratulations. Now you'll write it again. What you have is good, imperfectly good, and within its imperfections are the possibilities of finding something more satisfying, both for your reader and for you.

If instead of a book this were a course in revising academic prose, the catalogue entry might look something like this:

Writing 316: "Writing as Revision, Revision as Writing." How to think about writing as you write. As you red-pencil your way through a draft, do you know why you're doing it, what you're looking for, and what you hope to come up with in the end? *Requirements:* attention, patience, a complete or nearly complete draft of a work in progress. Anxiety optional.

The course would be partly a philosophy of written communication geared for scholarly writing and partly a set of strategies for tricking yourself into finding out what you think.

An open secret: it's OK to be scared by the responsibilities of writing and revising, at least sometimes. Many ideas fizzle, either because the writer can't concentrate on them long enough to blow a spark into a flame, or because the idea itself doesn't have the strength to become more than a hunch. So let's work with the anxiety. Use it to ask your text what it's doing and why.

"Wait!" (Reader looks again at publisher's description for *On Revision*.) "This sounds like it's about writing, not revising. I need to *fix* something, not make something from scratch. What's going on?"

As we all say in the classroom, "Good question." It would be hard to pretend that this is a book about something called revising that's separable from the thing we call writing. So I won't.

WRITERS ARE REVISERS—AND LEARNERS, TOO

Regardless of its genre or form, writing gets better when the writer goes over it again. Revising doesn't just neaten writing up. When you revise, something *happens*. Just as something happens in a classroom. In *The Missing Course*, David Gooblar observes that today,

> we understand that learning is much more like an act of revision. All of our students bring to our classes certain ideas about the world, and about our subjects, and these preconceptions are a crucial part of the process of learning new ideas. For a student to be taught, she must revise her current understanding to become a new understanding—it doesn't just happen automatically.[1]

1. *The Missing Course: Everything They Never Taught You about College Teaching* (Cambridge, MA: Harvard University Press, 2019), 17.

Gooblar's advice about teaching speaks to the writing process, too. Revising can be a pretty powerful metaphor for learning.

The nub of that theory of teaching—that it's about helping students to re-understand something, which is to say helping students to understand themselves in new ways—corresponds to a theory of writing: revising is re-understanding. Not merely re-understanding what you're writing but also re-understanding, by extension, your relation to a set of ideas that are moving through what you have put down on paper. At least in part, we are what we write. As you revise your text you'll be revising some part of yourself, too.

This drive to tinker, reshape, rebuild, and improve is partly deliberate, partly automatic. Sometimes we revise without thinking, because we know instinctively that we could do this or that better. Sometimes we revise deliberately, consciously, as a cycle in production. "Good news!" your inner writer teacher whispers. "You've reached the revision stage!"

In his classic (venerable isn't too strong a word) book *On Writing Well*, William Zinsser shares a feeling you might have experienced yourself:

> Learn to enjoy this tidying process. I don't like to write; I like to have written. But I love to rewrite. I especially like to cut: to press the DELETE key and see an unnecessary word or phrase or sentence vanish into the electricity. I like to replace a humdrum word with one that has more precision or color. I like to strengthen the transition between one sentence and another. I like to rephrase a drab sentence to give it a more pleasing rhythm or a more graceful musical line. With every small refinement I feel that I'm

coming nearer to where I would like to arrive, and when I finally get there I know it was the rewriting, not the writing, that won the game.[2]

That's the feeling to aim for, and to enjoy when it happens to you.

Sitting at your computer screen, though, that feeling may be elusive. It's just you, going back over a draft alone. Or maybe you get outside eyes to look at what you've done. You take to heart the encouragement and the critique, and you return to the screen and to your words, one more time, to make the draft just a little better.

To be honest, I don't feel I've ever written anything that entirely hit the mark. Even after multiple revisions, even after the book or the article has been published, I find ways it could be made stronger or clearer, bits I might tweak yet again. One reason not to look at your work once it's in print: you can't revise further, so why bother?[3] I take comfort from more than one celebrated actor who's revealed that she never sees the movie she's in for just that reason. It's done, and anyway there are other projects. It's OK not to reread one's work when it's *done* done, but revision is the crucially important process by which you get your work to that point.

Honoré de Balzac, the tireless nineteenth-century French master who lived on coffee and writing, left behind revised page proof of his 1833 novel *Eugénie Grandet* (figure 2.1). I love this document, now housed in the Morgan Library. Look

2. *On Writing Well: The Classic Guide to Writing Nonfiction*, 30th anniversary ed. (1976; New York: Harper Perennial, 2006), 87.
3. Did someone say, "What about revised editions?" Indeed. But those are the exceptions. Revising a published text at the publisher's request is a particular kind of revision, usually limited to necessary updates and corrections, and sometimes a new chapter, but rarely entailing a wholesale rethinking.

2.1 Honoré de Balzac, *Eugénie Grandet*, signed autograph manuscript and typescript with manuscript revisions, fol. 31r., 1833. Morgan Library & Museum, MA 1036; purchased 1925.

at the corrections! The rethinking! The intensity of engagement, the furious explosion of interventions, tell us more about Balzac's writing method than any interview a journalist might have coaxed out of him.

If you're hyperventilating at the sight of this sheet, you're not alone. Here's a writer who's sent off to press a text he may have already revised in manuscript. Now it's typeset but still a mess. A mess of improvements, that is: deletions, corrections, relocations, insertions. Balzac's revision mechanism calls upon all the pre-electronic rereading techniques at his disposal. Out of it come the words Balzac most wants to put out into the world. I don't know if he thought the result was perfect, but his proofs are testimony to his care.[4]

Two centuries on, and with the advantage of the digital tools at our fingertips, our task is surely easier than Balzac's. We can add, delete, or rearrange in a matter of seconds, erasing with a few keystrokes the version we now judge flawed and replacing it with what we're convinced is better. But how does that work? Does technological facility make us better writers? Better revisers? What impels, what guides our revising?

Let me jump to something that might feel as if it belongs in the last chapter of this book and offer an odd bit of anthropomorphism: we revise not only to find out what we really think or what the audience will accept, but to find out what the writing *itself* wants. Whatever writing's equivalent of a pulse might be, you want yours to have it.

4. A publisher might also hyperventilate looking at the Balzac sheet. Today, proof stage, even in digital form, is too late for such revisions, which are expensive, and likely to delay publication. It's typical for contracts to specify a small allowance for changes, beyond which costs will be charged to the author.

How differently might you think about your writing if you were to imagine your idea as an almost living thing that needs care, grooming, nourishment? A big, beastly creature you can never really "master" but with which you want to coexist?

When we write something that's worth the time we've spent putting it together, we haven't just arranged words nicely. We've also found an idea. If we've done it right, that idea has never been thought and said in exactly that way before.

The writing that works best feels as if it contains all the parts that are necessary and none that aren't. It moves along, presenting its idea, demonstrating the validity of an argument, dismantling a misconception, pausing to give the reader a chance to breathe and absorb what's just been said. For that to happen, you need to hear what you've drafted and to recognize when there's still work to be done. *Listen.* The ear—the internal, mental ear—is the reviser's most valuable tool.

In revising we want to protect what's special about that almost-living idea-thing. Revising is seeing what doesn't work, what doesn't belong. *Look. Listen.* Learning to revise means accepting that all writers—including the most revered, the most brilliant and influential—sometimes have lousy ideas or ideas that, good or not, just don't fit whatever is being written. That's why they revise. That's how they learn from their own work in progress.

ACOUSTIC READING, ACOUSTIC WRITING

So what's a writer in the twenty-first century? Here's a slightly wicked definition: a writer is a set of superb ears with adequate typing skills. Yes, thinking and arguing, sifting and shaping, are all part of the material of writing, but it's listening to what you've drafted that will make the difference.

Revising is going back to a piece of writing and trying to hear what's in the words you've got so far. What's missing, what's in the way, what's in the wrong place or in the wrong voice. What needs to be said, what needs to be unsaid (erased completely or, sometimes, just implied), what needs to be said differently.[5]

To do that we double down on our own areas of specialization, but we can also reach into our individual archives, study professional disciplines and forms of writing that are not our own, or explore metaphoric knowledge drawn from other fields and other sources.

Listening includes listening to things without voices. Geologists help us understand "what the rocks tell us" by examining evidence that shows how a rock formation came to be. Since the beginning of agriculture, farmers have known what the earth has to say. An ear of corn can tell us something about soil and climate change if only we ask the right questions with the right tools and listen carefully to the replies. A draft manuscript, which in its own way is as mute as a piece of schist or an ear of corn, can tell us things, too.

But writing isn't stone or vegetable matter. Writing is a paradox: it's mute, until someone reads it, and then it never stops talking. As writers, we want our talking-writing to say what it was meant to say, and we revise to make that possible. That's why we need to listen to our words—not just the words themselves but their layers and origins, their gaps and pauses, the big and small shapes into which they form ideas.

5. I've stopped counting how many times I've rewritten this chapter, or even figuring out exactly what counts as a rewrite. Each iteration, though, has been substantially different.

Want to be a better writer? Listen more closely to what the words do.

Writing turns out to be something collective, something that operates between you, all your experiences and ideas, and your sense of the writing you admire. That's all part of what we can call a *writing practice*. Your own writing practice is something you learn to do over and over again, repetitively and with adjustments, like gym warm-ups or keyboard exercises, or maybe the way birds learn to build nests year after year. You do this so language and ideas might stay in place long enough that others—unseen, unnumbered, unknown others—can engage with that language, those ideas. You want to write better so that others can read your writing better. You may write alone, in whatever space counts as your home office or in your version of a monastic retreat, but when you're writing well you're writing *among*, not alone. Not just *for* your readers, but *among* them.

Some writers draft and revise on paper, some on screen. How you work with your draft may alter your ability to hear it. I move through a draft more deliberately on paper, though my terrible handwriting is a challenge even to me. Can I hear my text better in hard copy? Maybe. I can spread a draft across a table, a floor, a desk, a bed. I can look at pages as if they're already in a book—a visual trick that offers a welcome bit of encouragement. But a physical manuscript demands that you work with its limitations. There's no search function, no easy delete key. In sheet after unalterable sheet, the writing unfolds slowly, saying what it has to say. Even in draft form, hard copy commands attention.[6]

6. Do we read more effectively on paper or on screen? Psychological studies suggest we may treat the on-screen document more superficially, racing along its seamless boundaries, because we can; paper . slows us, but also provides the reader with fewer distractions. On the

Revising on screen is different. A paper draft is locked in place. With an on-screen draft, you can keep tabs open, copying and pasting from other documents. Does that make the digital draft easier to work with? In many ways, yes. We've all internalized the bells and whistles of our favorite word-processing programs: our fingers dance over the keys, the text conforming to our specifications. And yet even the most sophisticated on-screen layout can feel like a poor second to those sheets of paper spread out on the surface of your choice. In either case, though, on paper or on screen, your draft is a text to be heard as much as seen.

Listening closely to your draft will tell you what you need to hear, but if others are willing to read your work and give you feedback, you'll have the added benefit of collegial or professional objectivity. That feedback is one reason that writing groups are so valuable. The other is, of course, that writing groups drive you to get the writing drafted in the first place. "I've promised my writing group partner that I'll give her a draft chapter by Thursday." These may be internal, extraprofessional deadlines, but that might make them more, not less, real. A writing group partner is a person, not a publication. Writing for a real, embodied reader may be the concrete motivation you need to finish up what a disembodied publishing house has expressed interest in.[7]

Some writers put off printing out a draft, as if hard copy

---

other hand, trees must be cut down to produce the paper on which we read, and much of that paper we quickly consign to recycling. See, for example, "Paper or Digital: Which Is the Best Way to Revise?" on the website of Avado, a UK firm specializing in "professional learning" in the digital environment (May 9, 2019), https://www.avadolearning.com/us/blog/paper-vs-digital-which-is-the-best-way-to-revise/.

7. Of course, a publishing house only looks disembodied. Try to see it not as an authenticating force in your field of study but as an organized team of professional individuals working together on their authors' behalf.

might jinx the process. ("It's not done. I don't want to see it 'in print' yet.") If that's your reaction to facing a printout of a work in progress, try plopping an all-caps running head at the top of each page: THIS IS A DRAFT AND I'M NOT HAPPY WITH IT YET. Or maybe THIS IS A STELLAR MANUSCRIPT AND I HAVE ONE LAST CHANCE TO MAKE IT AN EVEN BETTER ONE. That's a little loud, but it makes the point. I've used stronger language with my own drafts. In practical terms, of course, your project will have to be completed online before an editor will look at or even be able to receive it. A paper revision process is always going to be a paper-plus-digital revision process.

Even if you prefer to revise exclusively on the computer, seriously consider printing out whatever you're working on, at least once, at a fairly well-developed stage in the writing. What's a well-developed stage? When there's enough to go on but you haven't locked down every detail. Work hard to revise while you believe revision is still possible.

And then there are those very real, though invisible, human readers for whom you've been writing in the first place. This bears repeating more than once: however and wherever you write, when you're writing well, you're writing not just *for* your readers, but *among* them.[8]

TAKE GOOD ADVICE—AND LISTEN TO YOUR OWN, TOO

Don't just take writing advice; look for it. Frankly, the best way to learn about revising is probably reading a lot of good

---

8. In *Getting It Published* I made the case for *for*, pressing writers to amend a project's thesis statement to identify *for whom* they imagine a project is being written. I'm using *among* here to intensify that *for*, encouraging the writer to envision a readership not at a distance but within earshot. Get yourself in there.

writers in your field. That means reading very carefully (you've already been trained to do that) but in a special way. When you find something that strikes you as particularly well worded or argued, stop. Read it out loud. Read it out loud again. Copy it down.[9] Take notes. What makes it work for you? What's special about the way the words or the ideas are presented? What do you hear?

The more you can tell yourself about your positive response to good work produced by others, the closer you'll come to understanding what you're after with your own. If the published authors you read have done their job well you won't see much torment behind the words on the printed page. Don't be fooled. Revision comes with torment (though not torture). The people we regard as "good writers" sweat to get the right words on the page, and because they've done it, we can learn from them. Even so, most of us also turn to books on writing for advice. Here are a few that touch on the challenge of revising.

The Craft of Research by Wayne Booth and Gregory Colomb is a classic work for writers who undertake research. The authors lay out the principles of moving from the object of study to the product of study, and a lot of what they have to say is applicable to revision. They specifically devote twenty pages or so to revising research reports and similar prose work.

There's a charm to the conciseness of Booth and Colomb's advice on revising. A two-page section headed "The Quickest Revision" boils down a set of complex and reiterated engagements to this pithy summary: *clarity* is especially important

---

9. Do this and you'll be participating in the long history of common-placing, a practice at least as old as Seneca in the first century AD. With the arrival of movable type and printed books, commonplacing became a familiar reading practice. It's a good one, too.

at the beginnings of sentences and sections; *emphasis* is especially important at the conclusion of sentences and sections.[10] It's good advice, and brief enough to be memorized. You might also think of the work of a chapter, a paragraph, or even of a sentence in gymnastic terms: focus on the target and nail the dismount. It's natural to concentrate on opening moves, but dismounts are also crucial to effective writing.[11]

A different approach to thinking about revision threads its way through *Draft No. 4: On the Writing Process*, a book of essays by John McPhee, eminent nonfiction writer and veteran writing teacher. When you read McPhee you have the feeling that you're in a seminar, hanging on the unpretentious and completely serious advice of a writer who really knows what he's talking about.

Not everything McPhee has to say is keyed to scholarly writing, though. "Readers are not supposed to notice the structure," he advises. Well, why not? For McPhee, the structure "is meant to be as visible as someone's bones."[12] Understood this way, the prose fleshes out a concealed armature. That's artful advice for an essayist, but not always what the scholar needs in order to arrange ideas for a journal article or book chapter. Here's where professional and institutional differences come in. An essayist isn't usually required to compose an abstract to be printed at the head of the essay, but a scholar is often asked to do exactly that. The nonfiction essayist and the academic writer have a lot in common, but readers of scholarly work rarely complain that the structure

10. *The Craft of Research*, 4th ed. (Chicago: University of Chicago Press, 2016), 281–82.
11. Don't be surprised if gymnasts return in the book you're now reading. I love the idea of Simone Biles's athletic prowess as an ideal for writerly discipline.
12. *Draft No. 4: On the Writing Process* (New York: Farrar, Straus and Giroux, 2017), 32.

is clear and clearly visible. Scientific publications, for example, regularly summarize findings at the head of a few densely packed, data-laden pages.

So we need to emphasize a distinction between the kind of revision that a team of bench scientists must undertake and the kind of revision that occupies writers in most of the social sciences and all of the humanities. That distinction is the role of narrative. But it's not a simple either/or. For the essayist, narrative is an essential tool, however artfully and lyrically disguised, holding the writing in place; for the academic writer, argument and proof usually come first, and narrative is an afterthought. *On Revision* stakes a claim on the importance of narrative structure for academic writing. Don't worry if the idea of narrative feels like something they don't do in your field. They do. They just call it other things. Later in this book we'll look at how you might think usefully of structure as a means to narrative.

Kristen Ghodsee's *From Notes to Narrative* takes on the not small task of showing anthropologists and other social scientists how to take what their research reveals and make persuasive sense of it. The book's subtitle, *Writing Ethnographies That Everyone Can Read*, points clearly to its primary goal: readability. Ghodsee's book is brief, often colloquial, and encouraging. "If you remember only one thing from this book," she writes, "please let it be this: revise the hell out of everything you write."[13] I'd add that in some cases, the writer needs to revise the hell *into* overly well-behaved prose.

In her workbook *Writing Your Journal Article in Twelve Weeks*, Wendy Belcher provides timely and timed advice on

---

13. *From Notes to Narrative: Writing Ethnographies That Everyone Can Read* (Chicago: University of Chicago Press, 2016), 110.

producing academic prose. While the book is focused on journal articles, its insights into the terrors and challenges of scholarly writing also speak to the conditions of revising academic long forms. She cautions, for example, that an article abstract shouldn't read like a plan for work *about* to happen: "It shouldn't include statements like 'we hope to prove' or 'this article tries to analyze' or 'this study seeks to.' These are okay in grant proposals or conference paper proposals but not in a research article. An article abstract is a report on what you did do, not what you hope to do."[14]

That's a good point and addresses a problem common to undergraduate writers, graduate students, and professional scholars. The same unconfident author who declares what an article *will* do might be working on a book-length manuscript, announcing at the top of each chapter what he or she hopes to prove, or show, or examine. Whether you're working on an article or a book, a chapter or a scholarly essay, the process of revising requires deciding, knowing, telling, performing, convincing. Go easy on the hoping.

For decades, Howard Becker's *Writing for Social Scientists* has shared good counsel on what makes writing work, and that means, of course, what makes rewriting work.[15] I admire in particular his fearless championing of the short sentence. Because so much work in the social sciences is aimed at scholarly journals, Becker's deep experience with writing (a lot), revising (a lot), and publishing (a lot) is gathered here in on-the-ground advice that is not—hear me out, humanists—just for social scientists.

---

14. *Writing Your Journal Article in Twelve Weeks: A Guide to Academic Publishing Success*, 2nd ed. (Chicago: University of Chicago Press, 2019), 55.
15. *Writing for Social Scientists: How to Start and Finish Your Thesis, Book, or Article*, 3rd ed. (Chicago: University of Chicago Press, 2020).

You can learn useful and very different things about revising writing from these five publications.[16] If you write regularly, you probably have a small shelf of books on writing, on style, and on publishing, books that were written to help writers get to the next, clearer, more effective stage and to see their work through to print. Guidance concerning the revision of academic writing, however, tends to appear piecemeal, either as a dedicated chapter in a book of writing advice or woven throughout. It's easy to see why there isn't a shelf of books that focus exclusively on how to revise academic writing.[17] "Wise advice on writing" can feel as if it's either an index card worth of dos and don'ts or a subject too dependent on an individual writer's habits and inclinations to allow for useful generalizations. One is superficial; the other is a baggy monster.

We can, however, think about revision with the care we might bring to any other subject we write about. What's revision, anyway? Multiple iterations? Sure. Attention to structure, to how the work is laid out and proceeds? Yes. The sound it makes in the reader's head, the presentation of ideas, brevity? Persuasiveness, conviction, delight, shock? OK. Of course, different kinds of writing require different emphases, and different writers will set out different goals

16. If you're at the post-dissertation stage, you might consult, in addition to my *From Dissertation to Book*, 2nd ed. (Chicago: University of Chicago Press, 2013), Beth Luey's collection *Revising Your Dissertation: Advice from Leading Editors*, rev. ed. (Berkeley: University of California Press, 2008), which gives the reader (you) an opportunity to hear what scholarly publishers have been saying about doctoral theses and their possibilities.

17. Though there are some, and there will be more, different in how they understand revision and different in the guidance they offer. See, for example, the newly published *Revise: The Scholar-Writer's Essential Guide to Tweaking, Editing, and Perfecting Your Manuscript* by Pamela Haag (New Haven, CT: Yale University Press, 2021).

for themselves. That's as it must be, and there aren't any easy steps to guaranteeing a successful revision. How could there be? But we might still lay out ideas that can move each writer, working however she or he works, toward that better version.

SOME PRINCIPLES TO REWRITE BY

A lot of revising is taking seriously what you've known to be true about writing and are now ready to put into practice. Here are some principles, meant not as revelations but merely as reminders of what you as a writer already know. Everything in the chapters that follow will depend on these. You might want to read them more than once. Expect recognitions, not surprises, but if these pages help you sharpen your thinking about writing, this chapter is doing its job.

1. Correcting is not revising. There's no bigger misunderstanding about how writing gets to be better. Correcting is small, local, instant. It's essential, too, because nothing pops into the reader's eye as fast and sharply as a misspelling. This I know from ample experience with my own not deathless prose. (Howlers howl.)

Tedious and time-consuming, correction is mainly about rules. *It's, its. There, their.* What's as gratifying as a quickly fixed typo? If you've got an especially good eye for such tasks, you'll catch simple mistakes on one careful read-through. Or maybe you've had help from a teacher or a copy editor and are looking at pages marked up with shorthand like SFRAG (for sentence fragment), R/O (run-on sentence), or M/M (misplaced modifier). So now you'll fix them.

It's easy to confuse fixing errors with revising ideas and reconfiguring the shape of text. Not that correction isn't important. We've all been trained to live under the rule of Spell Check, a program that compares the words in your document with the lexicon stored in its archive and points out what it identifies as violations of linguistic rules. From time to time you might imagine there's an invisible writing teacher hiding in your laptop, silently nudging you to *Ignore, Accept, Replace All.* If there were a cargo cult for academic writers, the Spell Check deity might receive special veneration.[18]

Sometimes it's hard to draw a line between a tiny revision and a big correction. It's hard to resist the oft-repeated story about the writer who spent an exhausting morning taking a comma out of something he was writing and then putting it back in. The anecdote is often attributed to Gustave Flaubert, author of *Madame Bovary* and famous for the rigor of his writing process. The story properly belongs, however, to Oscar Wilde.[19] For Wilde (or Flaubert), the removal or insertion of a comma might really shift meaning and count as a revision (consider that instant classic of punctuation hilarity, "Let's eat Grandma"). Most of the time, we're likely to think of placing commas as a means of correcting grammatical gaffes or, if optional, as simply a minor matter of style. For our purposes, an inserted or deleted comma doesn't count as a revision.[20] Proofreading isn't revising, either. Revisers correct, then they think bigger. Proofreading is an essential last

18. Though like audio transcription, Spell Check can't really know what you have in mind. Let Spell Check bring things to your attention, but treat it more like a well-meaning busybody than the word police.

19. John Cooper assembles the evidence at "Oscar Wilde in America" https://www.oscarwildeinamerica.org/quotations/took-out-a-comma .html.

20. Of course, for a poet, every letter, every stroke of pen or type, is crucial. Scholarly nonfiction, though, has to think beyond the aesthetics of the microscopic. Don't write me letters.

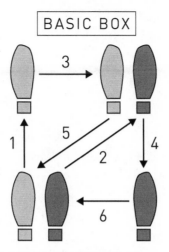

2.2 Dance step diagram. Photograph: Wikimedia Commons.

polish, and nothing like revising. Proofing stage is definitely not the place to "finish revising."

2. Writing is thinking—and for scholars, thinking means writing. Writing is what scholars do. Revising is a similar process—writing *as* thinking *as* writing—but done with a heightened self-consciousness that keeps its eye on the unknown, unknowable recipient of the text.

What were you thinking when you wrote that draft? Good revision is as much about the why of writing as about the what and the how of writing. It's not just your moves. A dance step diagram (figure 2.2) can only tell you so much about dancing, and a revision checklist can only tell you so much about revising.

If you want to be a dancer, dance. Even if you find that writing comes easily (at least on good days), revising is an order of business different in important ways from the process of putting thoughts on the page for the first time.

Squeezing big ideas into small spaces, or stretching small ideas over big spaces, reordering elements to make new connections, deleting things that once seemed important and now not so much, turning a page into a paragraph, a paragraph into a page. Or simply facing the harsh reality that what you've just written needs to be written again from scratch.

Poet and opium addict Samuel Taylor Coleridge, whose words often turn up on lists of wise advice about writing, is recorded as having said that he wished young poets of the day would remember his "homely definitions of prose and poetry; that is, prose = words in their best order;— poetry = the best words in their best order."[21]

Which is fine as far as it goes. If you're revising, though, it may not be enough to have a Romantic master's pithy admonition to find the best. You already know you want to find a version of your work better than what you have just now.

3. Good writing is persuasive writing. Whatever else they're doing, whatever other goals they hold dear, academic writers are involved in making the thing they have to say, in all its caloric complexity, strike their audience as persuasive.

Persuasion and polemic aren't identical, though they sit on a continuum. Polemic is the heartiest, most argumentative form of persuasion. The word comes from the Greek *polemos*, meaning war, and polemic is, in a way, war by means of language. Not all persuasion is polemic, nor should be, but all writers are in the persuasion business.

Most of what academics write is intended to persuade other academics of something. That's true for essayists, too.

21. Coleridge's son-in-law transcribed the poet's table talk (and published it as *Table Talk*). The remark is dated July 12, 1827.

James Baldwin, when asked if writing an essay was easier than writing a novel, replied, "An essay is essentially an argument. The writer's point of view in an essay is always absolutely clear. The writer is trying to make the readers see something, trying to convince them of something."[22] Essays, articles, monographs—the bread and butter of an academic writing life—are about persuasion. Those academic audiences are learned and demanding, and their curiosity is learned, demanding curiosity. They're trained to engage complexity (not just positions and speculations but also footnotes, endnotes, appendices, and bibliographical tails of all stripes). They live in expectation of argument and counterargument, of ideas in interesting shapes, laid out to pursue truths in new forms. They may read with their boxing gloves on.

Always acknowledge your reader and your reader's intelligence. Especially in the digital world, writing is less a delivery system than an ecosystem. This has been true for as long as writers have written with readers in mind. But the idea that writing is an ecosystem, with dynamic interdependent components, feels especially true in academic life. Understood that way, academic audiences are invaluable, not as recipients but as living components of an information network. "They" are "us" are "you": we who type away are writing for others as rigorous and skeptical as we are ourselves. That's how we all feed ideas and sometimes knowledge to one another. That's how we make new growth possible.

Like every other type of reader, scholarly readers want to be recognized by writers *as readers*. Embrace this concept and you'll figure out not only what you need to revise,

22. "The Art of Fiction No. 78," *Paris Review*, no. 91 (Spring 1984).

but also why you need to revise. Good writing understands that reading is more than simply getting information, or even being exposed to new ideas. Reading is an exchange of interest, not a one-way street.

Remember that readers want the writer's attention in exchange for their own. And who can quarrel with them on this point? Readers expect argument and persuasion, but that comes with risk, especially for us academic types, eager to press a point. Readers expect to be argued *with*, and persuaded *by*. They don't want to be told, repeatedly, what they already know, and they're rarely tolerant of being lectured *at*. Writing happens among; writing is an exchange.

I'll go further with this point, so bear with me. Readers aren't just people out there who buy, borrow, or download your written words. Readers engage with texts, giving them a life those texts otherwise lack. Readers, we might even say, *create* writers. They do this by creating the books that writers make, sort of the way a musician creates a piece of music by playing the notes the composer has set down on paper.[23]

There are other writing principles at stake, too. So-called creative writing understands better than most academic writing the importance of structure, voice, and story.[24] Those qualities are as important to the scholarly writer as to any of the creative writing genres, and they're as important to successful scholarly writing as is persuasive argument. Re-

23. Roland Barthes's 1987 essay "The Death of the Author" argued for the independence of the written thing from the writer. Barthes's sophisticated and widely influential claim resonates with *On Revision*'s modest injunction: listen to what the text does and says.
24. A sociologist, a literary critic, and a film historian plying their nonfiction craft are all creative writers even if they're not called that. In this book, I'll use the term *creative writing* as it's conventionally used. But I'm not happy about it.

vising scholarly writing needs attention to structure, voice, and story in order to achieve persuasion.

Persuasion isn't just a matter of evidence and footnotes. Not ever. They're just necessary details, compressed and placed to support but not to distract from the writer's main point. Readers focus on the body of the text. They want to know that a real mind housed in a real body produced something, that it thought about the structure in which its ideas are housed, and that it crafted an endpoint that delivers something. Even if you're working through an experimental mode of nonfiction, these principles apply. In short, readers want to know why they're giving their time to what you've written. Why, in other words, you're asking readers to participate in the ecosystem. As you revise, plan on having something for your reader to do and to work with.

To write persuasively, either as a student or as a professional, is fundamentally a matter of knowing, at last, what you mean. That, and figuring out how to prove it.

4. We live in a world of data and narrative. Our responses to argument and proof are conditioned by the systems within which we organize knowledge. By our disciplines, too. Evidence-based, theoretically driven work, generous in its curiosity, rigorous in its methods: that's a description of scientific inquiry, and it's foundational to modern life. So are the humanistic disciplines, for their richness, their connection to history, the attention they pay to people's lives, their tireless search for value and meaning.

Yet how often do we hear some version of the declaration that scientists use data and nonscientists don't, as if that definitively proves that science is real and true and other forms of inquiry and research can make no claim to those qualities? That impoverishing distinction, which sets the sci-tech fields and humanistic disciplines at one another's throats, has gained surprising traction in the twenty-first-century world. For those of us working in the humanities and much of the social sciences, there is continuous pressure to demonstrate that the methods of the nontechnical disciplines, whether wholly or partially qualitative, are as rigorous and demanding as those of the STEM fields are assumed to be. Mathematical proofs set a high bar.

And not merely high, but mostly wrong. For those scholars working in fields where "the book" is both the unit of scholarly production and the conduit of new knowledge, these are impossible standards, not because they're too high to reach, but because they measure other kinds of things.

The writing of scholarly narrative does work that the laboratory cannot. In 1949, the British philosopher Gilbert Ryle warned against the problem of the *category mistake*, sometimes also called *category confusion*. The repeated misapplication of quantitative tools to qualitative analyses is often, among other things, a category mistake.

To write effectively and persuasively, we need to know what the standards are in our field, what metric will be used to judge what we produce. So let's step outside our departments for a moment and think about how we identify ourselves.

Scholars and researchers across the disciplines might be divided into *data-driven researchers* and *narrative-driven researchers*. Data-driven researchers include most scientists, mathematicians, people working in technical fields like engineering, quantitative analysts in the social sciences, and, occasionally, even people in the humanities. Narrative-driven researchers are almost everyone in the humanities and that surprisingly wide swath of the social sciences in which analytic techniques and procedures are not restrictively based on data collection and analysis. So who counts as *them*? Who counts as *us*?

Those of us who write need a new term that can bring together the efforts of researchers, regardless of discipline, working in the narrative mode. Let's call the set of activities in which they engage *narrative analysis*. Not analysis of narrative, but analysis of any question or subject delivered in narrative form.

Narrative analysis is engaged in the endlessly complex examination of what people do and make and say. It does so with principles drawn from the humanities and social sciences, including logic and ethics, cross-checking and double-blind tests, principles that in turn help direct the ways in which questions are discovered and evidence identified. As writers, most of us are narrative analysts.

Redescribing the academy in terms of data and narrative might offer new opportunities to make connections across fields. It might also allow us to focus on the production of analytic narrative as a commonality binding much of the social sciences, most of the humanities, and even some aspects of the hard sciences. When you have something to say, and want others to hear, you order the pieces of your message to make that possible. That's a narrative.

Why is it important to focus on the narrative dimension of specifically scholarly writing? Because narratives tell stories, and stories interest people. Even scholarly stories interest people.

Data can, too, but most of the time we still need narrative to explain that data. Scholarly, analytic narrative tells complex stories about a complex world. It does this by organizing ideas, examining evidence, staging argument, and crafting language that can be taken up by its intended readers.

Or, to look at it from another angle, the academic writing we call scholarship is carefully researched nonfiction. Scholarship is writing for scholars by scholars about, well, scholarly things. But since scholars devote themselves to examining the world, life, ideas—everything, really—in pursuit of new knowledge, we have to shift the idea of "scholarly things" to "everything, once viewed through the tools that highly trained people bring to bear."

The object of scholarship is nothing less than new knowledge, and that means nothing less than the ongoing, unfinishable task of reimagining the world. The vehicle for communicating most of that new knowledge is academic work. That's the reason you're writing what you're writing.

5. Look for the good kind of difficult. Writing isn't ever easy, but it's just a bit more difficult for scholars, and that's the way scholars like it. Scholars live with (in, amid, for) difficulty because that's where thinking, and writing about thinking, is going to happen.[25]

That's not, of course, because academics are especially difficult people. You will know non-academics who are just as difficult as the most ornery scholars in your field. But scholars are people looking for trouble. They seek out difficulty. Where others see chaos or nothing, disorder or no discernible problem, the scholar sees the trace of damaged organization, unconnected points, even wrong turns, and within all that the possibility of exploration, the hope of explanation.

Scholarship is about explaining with new information,

25. George Steiner proposes analytic categories for the difficulties inherent in poetry. There are some appealing parallels between the work of poetic reading and the challenge of crafting a research project. See *On Difficulty and Other Essays* (Oxford: Oxford University Press, 1980).

new tools, new ideas. Good scholarship is always new, and always about the new. The scholar who works with fragments of cuneiform tablets is as committed to newness as is the scholar working to understand the mechanism of racial bias and voter suppression in twenty-first-century America.

Scholars get to that newness through difficulty, or rather through different kinds of difficulty. As you prepare to revise something, think about what makes your own scholarly work a challenge. There are dead-ends and trails that run cold, and doors that suddenly slam shut. There are many, many things we fail to understand well enough. There are languages we don't know and evidence just beyond the threshold of being decipherable.

How many forms of difficulty do you encounter in your work? You might recognize at least these:

the difficulty of disorder (the evidence doesn't make sense);
the difficulty of absence (the records were destroyed);
the difficulty of contradiction (two powerful traditions, two views that say opposite things);
the difficulty of not having the tools needed for the task (we haven't yet developed techniques for unrolling those papyri; the necessary archives are embargoed for another twenty years; and so on).

With difficulties come recognitions. If you know what kind of difficulty your writing project presents you with, you can think better about how to move it forward. Take, for example, the difficulty of disorder; your materials are in a state of chaos. That's an opportunity to recognize what you can and can't do. You can't make a finished project from a whirlwind of paper, but you can try creating a narrative from the things that you can organize, even if you know that there's too much to account for and assimilate.

Recognizing the difficulty of absence—not the disorder of evidence but its lack—compels us to speculate and theorize about gaps. That's a legitimate and necessary mode of thinking, as long as the writer acknowledges that these are speculations and theories instead of facts.

Recognizing the difficulty of contradiction cries out for a position outside and beyond any polarizing duality. It requires a new angle from which to observe contending forces and to think about them. Even if a contradiction cannot be resolved, it can still be identified and studied so that the next scholar to approach the problem might profit from your thinking.

Recognizing that we lack the tools to understand a problem, much less solve it, can reset the terms by means of which we think about that problem. Resets are critical to scholarly work. Defining what we don't know can be a writer's most precious gift to readers.

In revising, we want to clarify not only what we have to say, but the limits of what can be said. We revise not only to fill in the gaps but also to shape more clearly the arcs or units of our writing and the spaces between them, so that the prose is intelligible, so that what we have to share can in fact be shared. Take the task of revising as an opportunity to make the problem clear because, finally, the thing we write about, or explore, or struggle against—our *problem*—is the only real subject of scholarship.

6. We want the good kind of problem. Though we want difficulty, no writer wants the proverbial brick wall. The bad kind of problem doesn't go anywhere. The bad kind of problem often rehearses what's already known, or dresses up familiar knowledge with fancy neologisms, or involves little more than a small detail without foreseeable application.[26]

The good kind of problem, on the other hand, is a meaningful question that opens out onto other meaningful questions. When that happens, you've hit upon what we can call a *generative insight*. It's that moment when you can say, "I can see something others haven't noticed or understood, and if my idea is valid then a whole other set of questions, directions, even solutions might be opening up in front of me." What happens next is the process of moving *with* the problem to create something readable.

The generative insight is more than a good idea. It's an idea-engine that suggests new paths and creates lines of inquiry. We have other names for the generative insight: breakthrough, paradigm shift, game-changer. They're all ways to name the thing that's new, central, productive.

In scholarly writing, there are always little ideas and big ideas. We need both. Little ideas may be small but valuable corrections, but the big idea points the way and models how to think about something larger than its immediate concerns.

Whatever one's discipline, a scholar is trained to notice things, to prepare for those generative insights. That may be what scholars have in common: a capacity for sustained, responsible attention, even to the most minor things, informed by evidence, history, and a framing set of assumptions. A lens, a perspective, a theory. And something more: a desire to teach. Good scholarly writing isn't just thinking. It's teaching, too. A good kind of problem, then, is a problem that makes teaching possible.

26. Research into the bad kind of problem doesn't necessarily produce untrue conclusions; it might produce ones that are true but small and unuseful. You'll always know when you can aim higher.

7. Every text is a stage. Revising writing is work that takes place as a process of stages, and in at least two senses of "stage." You might think of revision as a journey, or as a moment along a course from point A to point B (think of a stage coach stop, or a stage in the growth of a person from infancy to adulthood). You already know not to "publish your homework," overwhelming your reader with things you've found or others have said. That would be pretty dull reading, however much you enjoyed doing the research. Imagine writing as a participatory activity.

A lot of us have been taught to think about writing, and revision, in terms of movement. Writing, and maybe especially the kind of complex writing that scholars produce, might also be thought of as a theatrical stage, a place from which the Actor (that's you, the writer) *performs the experience of thinking about something*. Staging your ideas is seriously different from simply encoding your research findings so that they can be transmitted to the appropriate parties for further analysis. I've just named two different, and legitimate, means of presenting what you know.

You can write about the same subject in many ways, of course, and when you do, you'll be choosing among several ways to stage what you know and what you want to say.

Here's an example. Dr. Ruiz completes a test concerning the toxicity of drinking water in Flint, Michigan. As PI on the project, hers is the first of eleven names below the title of the final report. The report is only ten pages long, but it's crammed with analytic and scientific detail, arranging and deploying data concerning the community's water pollution crisis.[27] It's a technical document, and it need not be written

27. As Lisa Gitelman and Virginia Jackson argue in the introduction to *"Raw Data" Is an Oxymoron* (Cambridge, MA: MIT Press, 2013), we imagine at our peril that data are somehow always neutral, transparent,

in urgent, sparkling prose. It probably shouldn't be. It's re-search, heavy on quantitative analysis, and written for other specialists in the field.

Dr. Lee is an urban sociologist writing an essay for the *New Yorker* that explores conditions in Flint, and the con-sequences of pollution on the work of raising kids without clean water. The *New Yorker* essay will not only deliver in-formation but also draw the reader into the experience of thinking about the subject—maybe only for the length of the essay or chapter but, each writer hopes, well beyond that, too. Dr. Lee may even draw upon Dr. Ruiz's technical report.

The two writers not only have written in different styles and with different degrees of detail, but they've also staged in different ways what they have to say to their readers.

To stage one's ideas is to organize and present them, and in that organization is a perspective, no matter how neutral or objective the staging aims to be. That's a kind of perfor-mance. Whatever you're writing, you're in there somewhere. Be as neutral as you like, as objective as you must, but you'll still be somewhere in your text. And it's a good thing, too.

We don't often talk about writing in those terms. It feels self-conscious, maybe even a bit narcissistic, to examine out loud just what *you* think about a subject, as if you were an-nouncing, "Enough about the pollution. Let's talk about me." But that's not what it means to perform the experience of thinking about something. This kind of performing is dem-onstrating convincingly why the ideas are important, what their origins and goals are, what your motivation in engaging them may be, and what you envision as their consequence. That's what's meant by staging your ideas.

---

inherently true. Data are selected and arranged to make an argument; in the sense we're exploring, data are always "staged."

Of course, these metaphors of staging are just that. The stage that concerns you right now is the condition of the text you're working on. However well organized, however systematic your writing and revising process, getting to your final version can still feel haphazard. It's not a science, but by going back through your text repeatedly, you will feel as if you're getting closer to the text *you* want to read and the text you want to share.

The experience of thinking about something—really thinking, creatively, with care and purpose—isn't always what we talk about when we talk about scholarly writing. And we should. That experience is more elusive than argument, more performative than critique, more elastic than evidence, but it's what happens when you write well and listen well to what you write.

The best writing, then, aims to create in front of a reader the writer's experience of thinking through a problem. It can be vivid, even gripping. Experienced writers do this through all sorts of tricks: shifts in tone and vocabulary, syntactic maneuvers and redirections of attention, quick moves from one subject to another, or settling in for something that takes pages of intense observation. When you're reading good writing, you feel that you're in the presence of a mind working something out, word by word, phrase by phrase by sentence by paragraph by page. Of course, not every writer has that skill, but it's an ideal to which committed writers, including committed scholarly writers, can and should aspire. As readers, we hang in there, turning to the next page and the page after that, listening to the writer speak to us.[28]

28. There are lots of ways to read, of course. Most of the time we dip and flip and scroll and risk making a hash of the best laid-out argument or the most thoughtful staging of ideas. But if what we're reading piecemeal seems worth it, we return to page 1 or scroll back to the top,

At the end of *A Midsummer Night's Dream*, the skeptical Theseus, who says he wants nothing to do with fairies and fantasy and artful language, complains that poets look at "airy nothing" and give it "a local habitation and a name." Theseus thinks he's applying his bullshit detector. Except he's wrong. There's a poetry in all writing, if by poetry we mean that crafting sentences and pages and chapters involves making a critical move: from ideas and many different kinds of evidence to something that's deeply concrete precisely because it's made of nothing more than words.

8. Don't undervalue instinct. Good writing, like great dancing, can't be explained simply so that anyone can do it. One of the truths of revision is that, after all the workshops and retreats and development sessions, everything one knows about writing is, finally, enabled by instinct. Great writers have it. Good writers have some of it. Most of us have a bit of it every now and then. People who call themselves poor writers think they have none, at least until they're shown how it's done.

The truth of instinct is felt everywhere. Just think for a moment about your own drafts, both the ones that work and are developable, and the ones that you know belong in a drawer. If you've been making that distinction among your drafts you're already putting your instinct to work. Anyone who writes will know the feeling that sometimes the piece being drafted may never get beyond draft stage, either because the writer doesn't want to take on the work of revising or because the writer isn't sure what the piece is, or both. That's instinct.

Some kinds of writing are really best as test drives, places

and start again. There's a tension between these two forms of readerly engagement. We'll look at them again when we get to the architecture of writing.

in which to spend five thousand words playing catch with yourself. There's no reason to take those pieces further. They're always going to be drafts, but may remain useful resources for better writing. I draft a lot, and I delete a lot. Just because a sentence is pretty doesn't mean it's true. And even if it's pretty and true, that doesn't mean it's useful to what I'm writing.

And yet. Every so often a writer drafts something that doesn't work but that offers a glimpse of a new start, a new direction, maybe even an entirely new and unanticipated project.

Good writing instinct will tell you that successful scholarly writing isn't about delivering information, much less (to let that antiseptic piece of corporate jargon into the room) "deliverables." Don't imagine—ever—that a writer is delivering content. That's what automated programs do, and many don't even do that. A writer demonstrates an idea for the reader. A good writer does it convincingly.

What *are* the best words, in the best order? How can we know? We work toward the goal of making a text speak what it has to say as clearly and as persuasively as possible. That's as good a definition of "best" as any I can come up with. Materials, stages, mapping, time, the presence of the reader: revision involves all of them hovering over you when you're revising something. You begin with your own work, reading it through, with eyes as different from your own as you can manage. You prepare to insert multiple queries into your online document or, pencil in hand, to make copious notes on your hard copy. Trust your instinct, because it grows out of experience.

9. Listen to others, even when it hurts. Listen as hard as you can to your own writing and to what you yourself have to say about it, but give special attention to external critique. Friends are great, and they'll tell you that they're there to help, but be merciful: not many people can or want to undertake a professional-level response to something written by a person they know well. "I really liked this" isn't an evaluative response; it's a pat on the back. If, however, you've submitted your work to a publisher and received anonymous, professional readers' reports, you're holding an invaluable preview of how unknown readers are likely to respond.

Scholarly journals and academic publishers depend on a commissioning or acquiring editor to be the first audience for your unpublished work. If it clears that hurdle, the editor may send it out for review. Rarely is a reviewer asked for a simple thumbs up or thumbs down. Reviewers are specialists with the training to make a useful, professional evaluation, often several pages long. When you get those reports, fasten your seatbelt, then read them with care.

Even the most enthusiastic specialist reader's report will come with some suggestions for strengthening an already strong manuscript. But some reports just say no. Responding to negative criticism is never easy. What writer wants to read that the project is misconceived or poorly executed? Trust me on this: unless negative critique is malicious (which rarely happens, no matter how bruised the author's feelings), the harsh reading is likely to be the toughest, most rigorous reading. Or to put it another way, the tough, negative reading is good when it understands and holds you to your own standards. Your editor will be the go-between, connecting you to your reviewers' reports, encouraging you to see the supportive observations but urging you to take seriously, and respond to, the uncomfortable points. So treat the engaged "negative review" as the toughest possible "positive review." Think of that reviewer as someone who wants to prevent you from making mistakes or publishing flawed work, not prevent you from publishing. A good editor will ask you to respond in writing to those critiques. Respond, not capitulate to. Read your readers reports carefully, decide what advice you can work with and what you can't. It's still your work.

*

So now let's pull these principles together and give them a purpose. As you write, analyze, and make plans to strengthen your draft, focus on the Three A's: *Argument, Architecture,* and *Audience.* No matter what you're writing, let these three targets be your constant companions.

First, *argument.* Don't get lost in the weeds. Know—really know—what you want to say about the thing you're writing about. An argument can't be about everything. Make it about something, and as specifically as you dare. Even if you aim to extrapolate everything from that something, you need a focus and a point. An argument is, first of all, a target.

Second, *architecture.* Understand the structure of the writing in front of you, think through the structure you need, and make those changes happen. Genres and fields have conventions. Know them, including the conventions for the shape of writing you're engaged in.

And finally, *audience.* Be honest about the readers your writing is capable of reaching. Write for them and bring them ideas they can use.

This has been a long, crowded chapter, but if you're taking your work from good to better there are a lot of things to be thinking about.

Drafts are better the second time around. One of this book's themes (to be repeated, because that's what themes are for) is that writing, and especially scholarly writing, is itself a kind of toolkit. Thinking of what you put on the page as a tool for your reader can transform your writing, both what you write and how you write it.

Now take a walk around the block or get a good night's sleep. When you're feeling fresh, the coffee is ready, and the desk is cleared, roll up your sleeves. That's the hardest part of writing, and it's the hardest part of revising, too.

3

Know what you've got

The writer Maggie Nelson offers an epigrammatic piece of advice about form and content: "Wait to see what you did to see what you did."[1] I think this means that you need to have done the writing before you can go back and discover what you've written, there on your own page. That's your ordinary, demanding job as a writer, finding out what you've got and deciding what you've got to do next. One of the hardest things about revising is knowing what you already have. Let's look at some of the ways to think about just that: seeing what you've drafted and how it got there.

So what kind of writer are you? How you answer may help you as you think about what you have and how you might revise it. There are slow writers and fast writers, writers who build from a central premise and writers who pull threads together to watch them develop into relations and connections. There are writers who work from a moment of inspiration without an immediate goal, and writers who imagine

1. Regan Mies, "On Writing and Pleasure: Zooming with Award-Winning Author and Poet Maggie Nelson," Bwog.com, Columbia Student News, October 2, 2020, https://bwog.com/2020/10/on-writing-and-pleasure -zooming-with-award-winning-author-and-poet-maggie-nelson/.

a grand plan before they've finished page 1. My best guess, though, is that most scholarly writers are either patchers or polishers.

Patchers work a paragraph at a time or a section at a time. A patcher gets as much of an idea down as seems possible. A long paragraph, or maybe two pages of thoughtful text. That's a patch of thinking. Then it's on to the next patch. In the Renaissance, fresco painters worked patch by patch, preparing a dampened section of wall and applying colors to that section. One day, an angel with a message; the next, a startled young woman reading a book. And so on until the fresco was complete. If you look carefully you can see the joins where one day's work ended and the next began. Some writers are like fresco painters, finishing off a portion of writing before moving to the next. Sometimes we can see the joins, too. If you're a patcher, you might have lots of files with bits you hope to use someday or today. A two-page burst that feels like a great question, a brilliant paragraph you haven't found a home for, a powerful quotation from an important source and your own equally powerful response to it.

Polishers, on the other hand, write something—sentence, paragraph, page—and immediately go through it again. And again. Moving a clause, replacing a word, refining the shape of a sentence. Polishers are never quite satisfied. They can always see room for improvement.

Polishers would be terrible fresco painters, but they might be excellent puzzle solvers. Patchers might be writers who can more quickly see what they want to accomplish, at least step by step. Polishers go back over their work, or can, so maybe here the right analogy is to artists working in oils, able to complete a canvas and set it aside, then go back and touch up the background, painting out the distracting extra figures and moving a mountain or two. If you look closely at an Old Master painting, you can sometimes see where the artist made a change, a place where the aging pigment reveals a *pentimento*, the ghostly shadow where a leg was once positioned or the distant house where a tree now stands.

Patchers might have a more instinctive feel for shape and more confidence in what the writing task requires. Polishers might believe in endless improvability, and that can be the spur to making good writing even better.

Each way of writing comes with its own cautions. Patchers can take for granted the reader's capacity to move with the writer from section to section. Transitions can be underfed. Polishers can take for granted the reader's capacity to see the forest in which the beautifully groomed trees have been arranged. Polished writing can sometimes be described as lapidary, meaning cut and buffed the way a gemstone is cut and buffed.

The distinction between writers who patch and writers who polish is only a small bit of writing theory. Real writers (you, for instance) do both. When you come to revise your text, though, it's helpful to be able to tell yourself out loud what kind of a writer you are, what your processes are, what your objectives are.

I'm a messy reviser. I work on sections and drafts that I've written but then can't connect them to one another. I'm best at fragments, but who would want to read my fragments?

I'm a messy reviser. I bolt through a draft so that I can get my ideas down and then I print the draft out and begin writing all over it in different colored pencils.

I'm a neat reviser. I work on sections and drafts and I connect them. Then I become a messy reviser and pull them apart.

It's a time-honored cliché that talking to yourself is a sign of madness. Don't believe it. What's writing, after all, but a process of talking to yourself in the presence of imaginary others?

HOW TO REREAD YOUR OWN WORK

When you revise you're noticing new things in your writing, things that want changing. I've said elsewhere that revision is a job for optimists.[2] That optimism can shine through in many ways. Sometimes it's hard to tell where writing ends and revising begins. Let's say you write Sentence One. Two minutes later you change one word in that sentence. Is that revising or just writing? Or you finish writing an entire chapter, break for lunch, and dive right back into what you've drafted only moments ago, listening for what might not quite work yet. Is that revising or just a good writing technique?

Let's look at your process again. You finish a chapter and put it away for a month. Now you reread it with fresh eyes and see that it's got terrific ideas, but they emerge only on page four, after three pages of prepackaged disciplinary truisms. You cut the truisms and the chapter suddenly has an electrifying energy, which you can ride all the way to the conclusion. Is that revising or just a good writing technique?

The two paragraphs you've just read might suggest a distinction between *continuous, ongoing revision* and *staged revision*. The difference is in the time scheme and in your intention. You did it on the same day, like the fresco painter who has to finish before the plaster dries. Or you went back some time later and saw from a fresh perspective what you

2. *From Dissertation to Book*, 2nd ed. (Chicago: University of Chicago Press, 2013), 27.

had laid down on the page. Immediate or delayed, uncon-
scious or deliberate, revision is something ongoing, something you continue, something you start. It's just writing.

The title of this chapter is meant to emphasize the continuum between the work you've done and the work you're
taking on. Revising isn't taking something terrible and
making it acceptable. Why waste time trying to revise work
you believe isn't any good? No, the work you put in front
of you *is* good, or has good things in it, what realtors call
"potential."[3] Never work from a draft you hate. Never work
from a draft you don't respect. Nothing worth your efforts is
likely to come from that labor. You need energetic commitment, and that's got to come from belief in the good—the
buried, damaged, confusing good—right there in your draft.

Bestselling author Daniel Kahneman published *Thinking,
Fast and Slow*, a book that brings into focus a set of problems
we all encounter in everyday life.[4] Honored for his work in
economics, Kahneman is a psychologist. The nub of the book
is an insight into two ways of thinking: quickly, based on
emotion and intuition, and carefully, based on evidence and
judgment. *Thinking, Fast and Slow* has been widely read and
discussed for what it explains, in ordinary language, about
intuition and decision-making. Kahneman doesn't focus on
revision, though the mental activities that go into revising a
piece of writing share characteristics with the processes and
procedures he describes.

What might it mean to set yourself the task of revising,
fast and slow? Might thinking about writing in those terms

3. Maggie Smith's poem "Good Bones" uses the trope of the realtor—
"this place could be beautiful"—to reflect on what we say to our children about the world we will leave to them. In finishing this book about
revision, Smith's poem was often on my mind.
4. *Thinking, Fast and Slow* (New York: Farrar, Straus and Giroux, 2013).

help make visible the ways in which we put our ideas down—the first time, and then again? Our assumptions, our belief in getting something important on paper, our commitment to analysis, correction, and discovery, but also our occlusions, the ways in which it's so easy not to see what we've written out in words. Easy not to see that our argument isn't quite an argument, or that the materials we've assembled are a stage or two short of being ready for a reader.

Revising slow might mean all the painstaking, reflective work this book encourages you to take on. Give yourself enough time to cook the material, to let ideas simmer. It's possible to produce *a* revision of something that just isn't *the* revision you're after. Keep at it, but give yourself time to breathe, and sleep, and do additional research if that's what you've discovered you need to get it right. Writing isn't a machine, and neither are you.

Revising fast could mean doing a revision quickly, which is almost inevitably going to be second-best at best. But revising fast could also mean giving your work a fast-paced read-through—no corrections allowed, no pencils, no breaks—just to see if you can feel the shape and the tone and come away with an argument.

It would be a generous friend or colleague who would help you test out your draft in this "revising fast" exercise:

Take your draft, estimate how long it would take to read at normal pace, then cut that time in half. Now turn to your generous friend. "David, can you read this for me in x minutes? Tell me what it's about."

You'll be asking David to speed through your prose—not at all the way you want readers to study your writing, but in practical terms that's how much hard-won prose may reach its readers.

Listen to what David says. Take notes. Be appreciative.

When you look back at your text, compare what your generous reader thought it was about and what you want the text to say.

There are other ways of using outside readers, of course. Asking persons with specialist knowledge is the most familiar strategy for crafting a safety net. Maria is a leading scholar in your field and also a colleague willing to go through a chapter, maybe more. Maria will read slow, not fast, taking all the time she wants, in order to give you corrections and to raise questions. Take notes. Be appreciative. Maria's responses are going to be close to those of a publisher's outside readers, who will also read your prose slowly, looking for faults, strengths, and more faults.

Many of us are fortunate to have Marias and Davids in our writing lives. We revise on our own and we revise with the help of others. The start button gets pressed often. The writer who waits for professional-level reviews is hoping for the best but should still be planning to revise as necessary. Reader reports often toss the writer back to the revision stage. It may feel as if you've bounced back to square one, but you haven't. This isn't failure. Not even a little. Why? Because the version that earned the readers' reports, and the opportunity they enable, wouldn't have happened had you not first done the hard work of pushing a good draft to be a better draft. With readers' reports you'll push a better version to be a still better version.

This artificial distinction between revising in response to others' comments and revising in response to one's own perceptions is just a schematic representation of how written work is made, is improved, and makes its way into print. In practice, any writer revises continually, seamlessly, letting the cursor backspace through one word choice and the keyboard summon up another. It's just writing. The changes we make as we write hardly seem worth noticing, but they're the heart of what writers do.

Find a quiet space you can work in for at least an hour without interruption, a chair you can sit in comfortably, good light, something to write on, and something to write with.

Boot your device. Open your file. If you can print out your text, have it by your side. When is the best time to revise work? When it feels almost complete but not locked down. It's hard to revise something that feels as if every inch has been polished to a high gloss. There's a sweet spot where revising a text feels most possible, a spot where changes can be most productive. There are lots of ways to read a draft. Beginning from page 1 will put you exactly where you imagine your reader will start. Read slowly and out loud, and listen carefully, both to what your words are saying and to how they're saying it.

But that's not the only way to reread; straight through may not even be the way that gives you the most useful insights into what you've put on paper. If your text is short enough, no longer than a chapter, you can perform the "reading sandwich": read the beginning, then the end, and only then read back over the big middle. The sandwich technique lets you focus on the first and last gestures of your text, the pitch and the closer. Those are the points your reader will encounter first and last, the enticing opening and convincing wrap-up. They're worth special attention. A caution, though. The "sandwich" technique can be an eye-opener with brief texts, but it becomes unwieldy with longer drafts.

The more complex the structure of your text, the more rereading options you have. And the more incentive to break your text into digestible units. Deploying subheads can make it easier for a reader to follow your train of thought, and they provide some breathing space. Use them. It can be a long swim from the beginning of your draft to the end, and you don't want your reader to give up on your prose (or drown in it).

Subheads alert, describe, consolidate, remind, and sometimes deliberately catch the reader off guard. Whatever your reasons, you're setting out a sign for your reader: here's a turn, get ready for something different. The judicious use of subheads doesn't just mark pauses and crossroads for the reader. In shaping the text into semi-autonomous units, subheads also benefit the writer. Like all signage, they announce something. So what do your subheads announce?

Depending on how sharply you define your borders, the text following a subhead can stand as a miniature essay or chapter. Once you see that structure facing you on the page, you can turn to a chapter's subunits with the same attention you would bring to the whole draft.

There are a number of subheads in this book. They carve longish stretches of writing into smaller pieces in order to make each chapter's points more easily useful for the reader. If you use subheads well, you'll be creating little subunits or essaylets within the larger structures of your prose.

Subheads are structurally useful in revising a text, too. They make it easy to reread by "leapfrogging," jumping from the draft's opener to the start of the section following the first subhead, then skipping to the next subhead, and the next, until you reach the end of your text. Reading in this way is a supplement to, and not a substitute for, the slow and careful rereading from page 1 onward. Leapfrogging provides a quick, schematic survey of the big picture. It's a bird's-eye view, too far from the object to resolve details but close enough to see the monuments on the ground.

Or you can reread by starting at the end. The best revisers know instinctively that the end of a text can be just as important, if not more, than the beginning. If that's true for your draft as a whole, then it's true for every paragraph in every section, and just possibly for every sentence. As you read backward, you look for the hooks that link one unit to the one before it, smoothing out the connections from unit to unit.

Is it OK to have abrupt shifts? Of course. But you may want to reserve startling transitions for those rare moments when you really want startling transitions. If modern-day readers are unlikely to exclaim *Non sequitur!* ("It does not follow"), they'll still notice when a link seems broken. Maybe the writer lost the train of thought, or couldn't bear to delete a nice passage from the working draft. Links and connections won't guarantee the continuity that makes a piece of writing easy to follow, but you can depend on confusion when you leave out the links and connections your readers expect.

The most rigorous rereading technique of all may be to move through a text sentence by sentence, in reverse order, from the final paragraph to the first, concentrating on logic and the smoothness with which each connects to its predecessor. Be warned: that's an exceptionally demanding exercise best reserved for short texts.

There are other rereading techniques, too. Ever write a note to yourself about your work in progress? Scribbling "This is great!" "Does this go here?" or "Check ref" is usable, concrete evidence of readerly attention. Go ahead; move through every page of your draft, noting its content and purpose. Those notes will add up to a kind of summary of your work in progress. It's a useful teaching technique when working with students, and it's useful for professional-level writing. Organize these page-by-page comments and you can generate a reverse outline of your draft.

You may already know and work with the reverse outline:

it's not the frame you build from which to write but a frame derived from what you've already written, a series of summaries or statements about where your draft stands. This is what paragraph 1 is about, this is what paragraph 2 is about, and so on until the end. Each of these methods can show you—more clearly, and maybe for the first time—what you've already written.

That's a short overview of some of the ways to reread. They all assume, though, that you know what you're writing about and why, that you've thought through the possible ways of proceeding, addressed pertinent objections, and are confident that your draft is moving down the right path. A piece of writing that's long or complex or both can be thought of in lots of ways; you can focus on its subject, its take, its extent, the chronological span, a theoretical or methodological model, a shape, a form, an imagined reader. These aren't just elements of what you're writing; they're also ways of looking at what you've drafted. A chronological approach, a thematic approach, a theoretical approach, an approach that highlights competing methodologies. Remember that your reader will consider the approach you take to your subject to be a choice, and as much a choice as your selection of the subject in the first place. What about your choices will make clear to your reader what you want to communicate? What will work best? And why?

Preparing to revise means facing what's important to you, the writer. The answer can't be "everything!" Don't aim for "everything" (which is often a stand-in for "I'm not really sure"). Aim for something specific that you can articulate. You're crafting a narrative to present an idea, and that idea is not only information and argument but also a tool.

That's why moving through a text is easiest when the writer asks the big questions. *What's the point of this? Why is that here? This looks like a diversion, but is it? Why another example?* A writer's questions are also a reader's questions.

So now the hard part. Starting a revision is only going to be as useful as your knowledge of your own process, your assumptions, your goals, even your blind spots.

Remind yourself of what interested you, what you wanted to explore and clarify, where your ideas put down roots. Why you're writing this thing at all. Remind yourself of what roads you didn't take and why. Roads need maps. A map of your writing can show you what you already have and give you ideas about what you still need. We'll get to the writer's map in a moment, but let's look first at the writer's archive, and then at a few ways to analyze what you have.

THE ARCHIVE OF INFORMATION
AND THE ARCHIVE OF IDEAS

You know what an archive is: a messy, organized repository of records with gaps, and fragments, and many, many questions. As you do research and take notes, you're assembling an archive. You're building your own *archive of information.* In the quantitative social sciences, the archive of information will give priority to data arranged in many different formats and from many different sources. In the humanities and narrative social sciences, the archive of information houses many kinds of information, though priority is usually given to what can be put into words, and is often exactly that: other people's words, with all the complexities of language as part of the territory.

You're also working with a second, intangible archive: your own imagination. It's the totality of your thoughts, theories, hunches, suspicions. This is your *archive of ideas.* The archive of ideas is the wealth of thoughts you as a writer have *about* the archive of information that you as a researcher have compiled.

The two archives are, of course, related. As a writer, you use both archives as you make your way through your own writing.

Using any archive requires discipline. However interesting your discoveries and insights may be, not everything you can research will deserve further attention. At the same time, not everything you *think* will in fact be worth the time. Nobody ever promised you that writing was a world made of straight lines. You might even have been warned that writing is more about loops and angles than straightaways. Yet out of your loopy, angled, un-straight draft, you want to make shapes that your reader will understand and be able to follow. That doesn't mean ironing your prose to flatness, but it does mean being in control of the direction of ideas and the shapes in which you present those ideas.

Archives are there to be studied, then organized, then tamed. Treating your own writing as if it were the consequence of both archives—the archive of information and the archive of ideas—can help you see the *relative* value of disparate materials and perceptions.

So what's useful in your archive? How big does an idea have to be? It's easy to think that you've got to have one big idea. True, a big idea does help a lot. But books don't necessarily come into being riding high on the Big Idea wagon. It's just as possible to have a lot of small ideas, and then see them gather steam and lead you to discover a big thesis you couldn't have come up with at the start. A lot of the kind of writing we're thinking about here works just that way.

One small idea animates a paragraph, another small idea animates another. The paragraphs build as the ideas build, and together they begin to create a network, a fabric of thinking that develops a chapter, a sequence of chapters, a book. At the end of writing out a full draft—and sometimes even before you finish—you may discover the ideal way of summarizing your thoughts about whatever it is you're writing about. You can't have the best possible description of what you're writing until you've at least finished a draft of the whole thing.

The larger the archive, the more discipline you will need to navigate, select, prioritize. The more noise, the harder it is to hear what's important. Archives are crowded places. Try to find the smallest unit of real importance—it might be the key document, the simplest formulation of a theory, the most concise and elegant question—and put it somewhere where it will always be close to the front of your mind. On the desktop, on a pad you keep visible at your workspace, on the refrigerator, even in your file as a tiny running head. Let it be the symbol of what's important to you in your developing ideas.

The archive of information is *never* the same as what shows up in your manuscript. It couldn't be. That would simply be writing down all your homework. Instead, you select, reveal, question, develop, arrange, even argue with material in that archive.

Remember the rules of archival research, because they will in turn become the basis for the architecture of whatever you're writing. You're expected to read everything but quote just what you need. That principle applies to your own ideas, too. Select. Use just what you need for this project, and for this revision. Of course, the best books are built on and out of more information than the author shares with the reader. It's less obvious that the best books are also built on more thinking about the subject than the author shares with the reader.

That's the trick of making scholarly research and writing work: everything and just enough, the comprehensive and the selected. And because it's true of writing it's even more true of revision.

Now try it. Reread the first five pages of your project. This is where you locate yourself, the problem you're exploring, and where you've imagined your reader. That's right. You're not just laying out an argument and delimiting the acreage of your project. You're also inventing your reader, sentence by sentence, and you're inventing one version of yourself, too.

An open secret of writing: those first five pages of your own writing are more important than the vast archive in those institutional boxes or in their electronic repositories. There will always be someone else who can open the boxes or spend months reading hundreds of PDFs online. The archive of information isn't going away. You, on the other hand, are here for a while, and your ideas are your own and only your own. Those five pages are the cornerstone on which you'll build everything, including your idea of the person who wants to read your work.

BE ANALYTIC

In his 1895 case study of Bertha Pappenheim, the Viennese patient who would become better known under the pseudonym "Anna O.," Freud's colleague Joseph Breuer worked through one of the most famous psychoanalytic analyses ever committed to paper. But it was the patient herself, Fräulein Pappenheim, who gave posterity the case's most memorable phrase when she referred to Breuer's procedure as "the talking cure." The term has become part of culture.

Less famous, though, is the other part of Pappenheim's analogy. She also called the psychoanalytic process "chimney sweeping."[5] Imagine now the draft as the patient, and revision as the writing cure. And yes, it involves sweeping out ash and soot.

This kind of sweeping isn't easy. It's understandable if you're seized by the urge to begin with a red pencil in hand and page 1 laid out on the dissecting table. Stop. Don't even think of rewriting your first five pages until you've read all the way to the last five, or at least have a confident sense of what the entire text does. If you haven't reread your draft in a month or more, you need to go through it again, in full or in a slow skim, before turning back to those first five pages.

This may make obvious sense if you're revising an article or essay, but it's true about book-length manuscripts, too. That means a lot of reading before you sit down to revise chapter 3. The rereading preparatory to good revision is critical. If you're going to connect chapter 3 to its siblings, you'll need to hold as much of the book in your head as you can.[6]

As you reread your own work, take notes. Lots of them. For now, put down the scalpel, and the broom, too. Think not only in terms of content and ideas, but of objectives. Scholars are good at analysis. Make the effort to analyze your own writing.

What kind of discipline makes the best revision possible? The legal philosopher John Rawls famously offered a thought experiment in which decisions about justice would be made behind a "veil of ignorance." You would decide whether something was just or unjust without knowing who you your-

5. Breuer notes that Pappenheim said the second part "humorously." Try not to think of Dick Van Dyke in *Mary Poppins*.
6. An unreasonable standard? Not really. Copy editors have to do exactly that: holding as much of the text as possible in memory in order to catch the repetition of a point or a phrase.

self were. That is, you would decide without internalizing your own privilege and position, whatever they might be. Deciding whether an action is or isn't fair, then, wouldn't depend on your own experience or your own personal system of beliefs. You would be asked to decide whether something was just without knowing whether "you," on the other side of that veil of ignorance, were female or male, young or old, a parent or not, alone or in a stable relationship, African or Asian or European, a person of color or white, or any of the other ways in which we tell ourselves we have identities. Rawls's thought experiment finds a positive value in ignorance and pushes us to use it.

It would be a big ask to compare revising a draft of, say, a book-length manuscript to the momentous implications of Rawls's theory of justice and that veil of ignorance. But if you'll indulge our very own, very small thought experiment, you really will want to make decisions about your draft as if it were not "yours" but instead something written by a well-informed, remarkably attentive writer unknown to you. Good revision gets not only to the "what" question but also to the "why" question. It does it by looking at the draft as if it were *unfamiliar*. On the one hand, you need to know pretty much everything that's going on in your draft. On the other, you need to look at that draft as if it were the work in progress of Writer X, an unknown scribbler on the other side of a powerful writerly veil.

Objectivity, then, is important, but that doesn't mean you want to disappear as a writer. Instead, you want to write and revise as if your presence, however it's marked in your writing, isn't prejudicial to your argument. Strive to make the best, most persuasive argument, best fitted for your readership, even if your text is powerfully anchored to your own experience or position. But take special care to respect the veil of ignorance, to argue well, to tell the story well. A good veil is a surprisingly useful writing accessory.

So far we've complicated the process of revising what you already have in order to bring to the surface these two great and cooperative archives: your research materials and your ideas about them. Now let's think about organizing what you've drafted.

Some tools for thinking about your writing process are especially useful. Here are three: *inventory*, *keywords*, and *map*. Think of them as overlapping ways to tell yourself what you're up to.

INVENTORY

Organizing your ideas and your research materials is already a form of inventorying. Inventories are lists of things. Almost every nonfiction book has at least one inventory as its table of contents, and usually another as an alphabetical index. The book index makes no judgments as to the weight or importance of individual entries. In an alphabetical listing, *applesauce* is no less important than *Aristotle*, and even gets to come first. The book's index is meant to be read simply as a finding tool.[7]

A table of contents, which usually appears at the front of a book, is a subtler inventory, providing order and, implicitly, a trajectory for the reader. In early modern books, the table of contents—frequently called simply "The Table"—might appear at the end of the text, rather than the front, reinforcing

---

7. Or maybe not quite so simply. To create an index entry is to assign a term some readerly value. Complex indexes break a term down further, attaching page numbers to subentries. On the complex role of the index, see *Book Parts*, ed. Dennis Duncan and Adam Smyth (Oxford: Oxford University Press, 2019).

the impression that the index and table of contents we know today are genetically related.

Now let's look specifically at the draft you're working on and see how an inventory might help. Unlike a published book's table of contents or its culminating index pages, an inventory composed at draft stage is simply a reminder, a to-do-or-at-least-don't-forget-about list. The draft's inventory can be as simple as a record of components, or topics, or just things you want to make sure you've covered:

competing histories of American whiteness
Baldwin's understanding of white self-illusion
histories of failed activism as anti-activism

Just three markers for subjects of different size, but they act to remind the writer of the parameters of the writing project. Any writer can have a moment to ask, "What is this about, anyway?" A modest inventory acts as a reminder of what you had in mind and what you want to keep in mind. The more complex the writing project, the easier it is to get lost in the prose of one's own draft.

That's only one form of writing inventory. You might prefer an ordered sequence, as in an old-fashioned outline. Or a list of names or events. Or, again, a collection of things not to be forgotten (the Latin word *memoranda* means "things to be remembered," a handy reminder to write such things down). However you approach it, your writing inventory lays out components and emphases so that you can find them to build or rebuild your text.

Here's an intentionally messy example. In drafting an essay that might become a chapter that might in turn become part of a book about the history of flavors, a writer crafts an inventory of details and materials for further study.

The subject is the taste of liquorice. The writer jots down notes, briefly inventorying possible points to consider:

character of liq—the root is the important piece

Pontefract—the "broken bridge" town—home of liquorice? who knew?

the early history of Pomfret (Pontefract) Castle

any connection to the death of Richard II—1400?

what about monks or Crusaders—link of P with liquorice?

the combo of liq and sugar traced to the mid-18C—Pontefract cakes

Dunhill

what's appealing about the taste?

effects on endocrine system—how much medical in this essay?

Proustian memories

concerns about abuse of

distinction between liq and similar flavors, such as anise

the role of ammonium chloride in the final preparation

Scandinavian liquorice—the exotic salty sweet

This obviously isn't a structure, much less an outline. It's barely a set of notes. It's more like a shopping list or a set of points of interest for the writer to consider. As the writer goes about composing the essay, some of these points will be developed and others will fall away. The writer has some interests and curiosities, and now needs to pursue them and test out their value to the piece under construction. At this stage, the writer has no central question, much less a thesis about liquorice. There's work to be done.

Of course, if you're working on a professional-level essay or a full-length book manuscript, you'll be dealing with more than the question of how liquorice was grown in Yorkshire.

Adapt the principle of inventorying so that it helps you identify your memoranda, those things you must remember if
only to decide which ones you don't need to include. Write
things down so they don't fall off the edge of your desk and
out of your head.

An informal inventory might also look like a list of topics
and concerns and less like a list of future index entries.
Here's a topic inventory drawn up by our invented author,
Dr. Lee, writing about the water crisis in Flint, Michigan:

> *incidence of childhood illnesses prior to 2000*
> *incidence of childhood illnesses in 2014–15*
> *lead poisoning*
> *race and the allocation of state resources*
> *the EPA's failure to intervene*
> *the Flint River as industry's dumping ground*
> *children's health initiatives in Flint*
> *Concerned Pastors for Social Action*

Like the scattered subjects in the previous example, this
isn't quite a structure, but you can see more easily where the
essay might be heading. It's a list of things of importance to
the writer, who may add, delete, or rewrite these entries as
the writing and rewriting progress further. Not a structure,
but a place from which to see a structure. A set of concerns,
a point of view.

The figure of the inventory can also be used more directly
to tick off a set of ambitions for your draft. A manuscript in
the history of science is primed to tell a new story. This time
the writer is making an inventory of objectives for an article
on the life and career of Valdivia Blackwell, an overlooked
(and fictional, sorry) twentieth-century bench scientist:

> *make a case for Valdivia Blackwell as an important figure in*
> *plant genetics*
>
> *locate Blackwell's career within a tradition of female researchers*
> *whose contribution was subsumed into the achievements of the*
> *(male) team leader*
>
> *organize the evidence linking Blackwell to the development of*
> *the rot-resistant cranberry*
>
> *tell her story!*

Now you've named not only materials but also tasks, arguments, an objective. Use your inventory as a reminder, in writing, of what's important to you as the writer about the subject you're working on. *Tell a story.* As you revise, work to keep fresh in mind what's driving you, and how you want to share both some form of new knowledge and some idea of that drive. In short, whatever your project, don't forget why you're writing.

KEYWORDS

The inventory exercise is meant to let you find the significant points or themes in your project, and to get you to say them out loud. Large and small, if they're on your mind you need to grapple with them one way or another. Some will have to go, either because you can't flesh them out or because, having fleshed them out, you see that they just don't belong in the text you're working on. Some will stay and only become more important.

A less familiar way to review your work in progress is to determine what we can call its keywords. The term has become familiar in academic circles, but it wasn't always the case. In 1976, the Welsh social critic Raymond Williams published *Keywords*, a dictionary of concepts in which he examined the cultural meaning and valence of more than one hundred terms.[8] Williams's book became a model for other scholars seeking to pin down and explain the terminology that makes a discipline tick.[9]

You can use the concept of the keyword to help you revise. Suppose you're writing on evasive behavior. In your working notes, *depression* is a keyword, and you make a strong case in chapter 1 for its importance in your thinking. Chapter 2 seems to focus on *misdirection*. Chapter 3 uses the terms *denial* and *self-esteem* a lot. These seem to be keywords. Will your text read better if you draw your keywords across the chapters? Or might you be more successful if you isolate concepts within individual chapters? Use the technology. A simple electronic search of your document will call up each occurrence, showing you exactly where a term occurs and giving you an opportunity to adjust its frequency and placement.

First, though, you want to be sure you know what terms are key for you in what you've written. Make a list of candidates, and search for them. Do these powerful words occur where you thought they did? Do you say about them what you hoped to say? Will your reader see these terms as key to your study?

A keyword search is only as good as the list of terms you assemble, but it's a chance to see how you've distributed

8. *Keywords: A Vocabulary of Culture and Society*, new ed. (New York: Oxford University Press, 2015).
9. The Keywords series, published by New York University Press, and the Critical Terms series, from the University of Chicago Press, comprise essay collections organized by disciplinary field.

your ingredients. Of course, there's no rule that a keyword has to appear regularly, like clockwork, throughout a piece of writing. That would be mechanical and boring. But if you plan to discuss a crucial term in only one portion of your text, be sure you know why.

As you revise, take the opportunity to step back, to see what concepts and words you want to carry through the entirety of your text. Readers appreciate threads built out of reminders and continuities.

Here's another example of a writer working through an overview of a project:

> I'm writing a history of the polar environmental crisis that considers global warming as a means of reconfiguring how we understand and measure time.

The writer has built this tight summary description out of what seem to be her key terms: *polar* names two enormous and very different geographic areas; *environmental* and *crisis*, which are now unfortunately inseparable, gesture toward large concepts in our modernity. Then there's *time*. If this sentence accurately reflects what the writer is working on, this capsule description is marking out the parameters of the discussion to follow. A good start, and now it's up to the writer. How will the terms be deployed in the draft? Will they appear throughout, or only in two of seven chapters? Are these keywords threads that run throughout the work? That's looking forward. But what if a capsule description is written after the draft has been completed? Then the writer can read backward, combing the draft to see if the keywords are in fact deployed to do key work.

What words would be the keywords in your own draft? Making a list of a dozen or so can create a sort of constellation you can use as you develop your revision. If you like working with word clusters, you can use text mining and related analytic techniques to quantify and visualize the frequency and relationship of terms you want to prioritize.

Keywords can help you to keep the energy flowing through your writing. Think electricity. At the very least, knowing where your keywords are located will tell you where the sockets are.

MAP

Just as an *inventory* is a catalogue of elements (materials, ideas, emphases) that may or may not belong in the finished project, a *map* is a picture of what you've written so far.

The map works spatially. It considers prose as if it occupied space, which it does, whether on the screen or on the page.[10] Within that space are components: episodes, people, histories, theories, ideas. As you write, you manipulate these components, moving them through the geographic space of your text.

Your writing travels (remember the stages metaphor). Some parts of your draft are flat, easily crossed stretches of writing. Those are components you understand well and can effectively connect to what surrounds them. Other parts, though, can feel mountainous or broken by impassible canyons. How do I get from here to there?

Begin by numbering the pages in every draft of anything you're writing. Record the word count, too. Update this information at the end of each writing day. Don't worry that this might sound obsessive: make a practice of logging in a word

---

10. As well as temporal space (duration) and mental space, but for the moment we'll think of space in the most immediate, writerly way: the space of words laid out one after another.

count and date at the top of each draft, just before wishing your laptop pleasant dreams. *Oct 6th 8,604 words.* The date, the number of words in the draft. You'll tinker with a paragraph or two on October 7th and the word count will change. Update and redate the file.

You're working to specifications, maybe a 60,000-word limit in a contract or the 6,000–10,000 word parameter set by a journal. Your word counts are immediately important.[11] Even if you're writing without an intended destination, keep counting words. If you're tackling a book-length draft, keep a running tab of each separate chapter.

That's one way maps are built. Now you're ready to look into the text of your draft text itself. What are the borders of your project? Where are the dangers? Popular culture enforces the idea that ancient and medieval maps warned mariners not to sail beyond the "known" territories. "Here be dragons" (or lions, or monsters).[12] You will know where the uncharted territory of your writing lies. There's the part of the world that you need to explore, and the part that might be interesting but shouldn't become a focus of your current writing project.

Labels, markers, titles. The real work of mapping a draft begins with giving it a title. What's true of revising is true for writing the first time. Even at the earliest stage of composition, try not to settle for something like "an essay I want to

11. If you're writing to spec, you'll have detailed requirements from a publisher: cover this material, at this level, for inclusion in this volume or series, and so forth. Thinking about the revision process can help you meet those criteria, but the publisher's instructions shape your primary obligation.
12. Among the New York Public Library's treasures is the Hunt-Lenox globe, which dates from 1504, and is the oldest surviving globe representing the New World. It's famous, too, for bearing the inscription HC SVNT DRACONES, indicating areas unknown to the cartographer. The phrase "Here be dragons" has taken on a life of its own.

write about women's soccer." A working title insists on telling you something about your subject and how you're writing about it. "Compensation inequities in women's soccer" is different from "Hands off women's work." Either might be right for the right venue, but the difference between them is going to shape the way you write every paragraph that follows.

Now continue with mapping the draft itself. Doing that can be as simple an exercise as marking the natural breaks in your text. "Something happens here." "I'm moving to a different point in these paragraphs." "This section is my favorite part" (what's important at the moment isn't that it's your favorite; what counts is that you've identified it as a semiautonomous unit within the draft).

Do this a couple of times. Make artificial divisions in the draft text. Do that again. On a second or third pass you'll begin to notice that you're more, or maybe less, convinced of the divisions you're creating. Shapes and misshapes begin to emerge. You'll see repetitions and recursive passages, sentences from section G that belong in section D, and so on. When you think you've broken the text up into pieces that make at least some sense to you, give them names or labels. You can be tentative and playful ("Section where I argue with Foucault"), or serious ("The misunderstood panopticon"), as if you were trying subheads on for size. Which is really what you're doing.

Whatever you're writing, your topic will have borders. *I am writing a study of unemployment in this period, in this geographical region, in this industry, in this socioeconomic community.* The writer has just described or mapped the terrain of this analysis. The project does not intend to engage material outside this period, region, industry, or community except as supporting or comparable data. Its focus will be limited and enriched by that limitation. That's not about avoiding dragons, exactly, but by articulating what you're *not* doing, you develop a clearer sense of what you will be doing.

As you map your draft, read it out loud and try to hear shifts, the changing emphases, the new interests, emerging points of focus. Make notes for yourself about the shifts and differences. A shift isn't bad, and might be crucial, like a director's wanting a different angle and cueing Camera 2 to pick up from Camera 1.

When you notice a shift, stop. Figure out the angle you've just created and the section that the angle has made. Label that section. You may later drop it or change it, but once you've named a stretch of prose, you can think about that sequence of paragraphs as an element with its own obligations and capacities.

This "intermediate labeling" (yes, it sounds like a crafts fair event) is the simplest and most basic revision tool, so simple that we risk not taking it seriously. Some labels will be there only for a short time as you continue to move prose around, deciding what element goes where. Those that make it to the final cut, however, your reader may eventually see as subheads.

Take labeling seriously. It's a way not only to announce something but also to build up your knowledge of your own text. Say, for example, you insert this label on page 17 of your draft:

Community responses

That's a helpful beginning. You've identified a small island of prose. You can go on through the rest of the draft, finding places where another marker can be set down, each naming a small stretch of writing. At this point, it's not worth worrying about the size of the prose islands you've named. Some marked sections will occupy very little acreage—maybe only a couple of paragraphs. Others will go on for many pages. Don't worry if some of your marked sections are ten pages and some are two paragraphs. That will change. But make marks; try as best you can to identify the parts.

When you've gone through your text, giving name to all the bits that make up your draft, you've mapped it. You're at an important discovery stage. Does your text look different to you now? You'll be itching to rewrite those underdeveloped islands. Resist the itch. The discovery stage of revision should be a view from thirty-five thousand feet of the territory below, not a moment to land and repaint the barn.

After you've moved through your draft once, go back and move through it again, this time focusing just on the words that make up your intermediate labels. Try adding more words to those labels, checking to see if the subhead really does describe the section it leads. Don't be fussy; be descriptive.

Community responses—the cost of bottled water, food

Remember that no one is going to see your draft, or your revision, unless you want them to. So be expansive. You can even push back.

Community responses—how does this build on the previous section? Is it really "community" I'm talking about or particular officials from the opposition?

If that doesn't feel quite right, do it again. As you move through your text, adjusting and relocating paragraphs, you'll probably see that a label that felt right a week ago feels out of place (so move it) or awkward (reword it) or unnecessary (cut it). Revision's all about fluidity. Focus on process.

USE THE TECHNIQUES THAT WORK FOR YOU

Inevitably, you'll rely on instinct (that word again) to draw on whatever tools feel helpful *right now*. What may work for one revision may be too much, or too little, for another. The longer your project, of course, the more pieces and approaches you'll be juggling.

One final invented example. A writer in the field of early American history is revising, chapter by chapter, a book-length study of education in the colonial period:

> In this chapter, I account for the gap in our understanding of the concept of literacy in early America, present two explanations for the development of the current dominant paradigm (which I critique), and identify three lines of inquiry that can reframe the demographic and economic conditions within which a more responsive concept of literacy might be understood.

This very organized scholar has already inventoried her chapter. She's even done it in the form of a list of objectives. Our writer knows there are six things she wants to accomplish, and she's summarized them to herself in the short paragraph above. Her special concern is with what we don't know about this period in American history—and what we should do about that. This is how she sees what she's drafted so far:

1 statement of the misunderstanding
2 explanation #1 for the development of the misunderstanding
3 explanation #2 for the development of the misunderstanding

4 line of inquiry #1
5 line of inquiry #2
6 line of inquiry #3

"But have I got it right?" she asks herself. And that's the right question. Perhaps her thinking goes something like this. She might even have written these words down in her notes to self:

> Do I really provide a fair explanation of a view of the past as it has been widely accepted? Do I have command of the scholarship and the footnotes to demonstrate the completeness of my research and my sense of responsibility to earlier scholars? Do I really draw a significant distinction between my two explanations for the dominance of what I believe to be an inadequate paradigm? Since my argument involves economic and sociological perspectives on early America, am I holding myself to rigorous disciplinary standards and not smoothing out gaps in our fragmentary evidence just to make my case? I'm less concerned about the three forward possibilities because that's what they are—windows for others to look through. Double-check to be sure I'm not adding more complexity than this chapter requires.

Our writer is determined to find out what she knows and what she doesn't. She may conclude that line of inquiry #2, whatever it may be, pushes her study too far afield. She might determine that it's outside the map of her project. That's valuable knowledge. Line of inquiry #2 may be the beginning of an entirely different writing project, or at least an essay separate from the current draft. Each of those decisions and insights will be valuable as she works through her chapter. By excluding aspects of her topic, at least for the moment, she can clarify her immediate purpose and lay the groundwork for another chapter or essay or op-ed.

If she (being invented) can do this, so can your very real self.

NEXT STEPS

Now make the process your own. Analyze your draft and plot your next steps. Review your archive, think through inventory, keywords, and map: use these tools separately or together, in whatever way that they can help. See where they reinforce your most important concepts and arguments. Go back and forth, checking what this one tells you and whether this other one agrees or tells you something different. Use every tool available whether you're revising a single unit (essay or chapter) or a compound one (a book manuscript composed of multiple units). Because in revising, the point is knowing what you have—really have—so that you can figure out what's missing or what's there and shouldn't be.

Techniques and habits of working are sometimes described as a writer's "process." What's that exactly? Your process is whatever works for you. The legendary sportswriter Red Smith, who didn't go in much for prose dramatics himself, remains most famous for saying, "Writing is easy. I just open a vein and bleed."[13] You may even have heard academic types talk about spilling their guts on the page. Scholarly writing may be exhausting and demanding, but it shouldn't involve bodily fluids.

13. The remark may be legendary, but Ira Berkow's *New York Times* obituary for Smith attributes it thus (January 16, 1982): https://www .nytimes.com/1982/01/16/obituaries/red-smith-sports-columnist-who -won-pulitzer-dies-at-76.html.

Everything in this chapter has urged you toward self-analysis, or at least analysis of your process, your intentions, and your draft. Can I know it better so that I can say it better? Can I structure it more tightly and more clearly? Can I pull it together so that it's convincing and stimulating for my reader? Answer those questions for yourself and you'll have answered them for your intended readers. But don't trap yourself in a search for a perfect form, a perfect argument. Get to *better*.

There's a fairy tale (there are probably many) about a magic pot that is never empty, no matter how often the hero dips into it.[14] Believe in that magic pot. It will refill itself as long as you want it to. Trust yourself: you won't run out of ideas.

Sometimes the right sort of intellectual obsession can be the magic pot. Don't be too professional *not* to be obsessed. It doesn't work that way. What really gets your writing going is the fire in your head. The critic Eve Kosofsky Sedgwick rates "obsessions [as] the most durable form of intellectual capital."[15] You can do things with capital.

I didn't put Sedgwick's cagey observation at the beginning of this chapter for the simple reason that I wanted you to think first in more sedate terms about what you have. Two archives, yes, and one more important than the other. Inventory your work. Be sure you know what terms or concepts are especially important and whether they're doing the

14. Readers who were once children may recall Tomie dePaola's Strega Nona and her magic pasta pot, a Calabrian variant on the global figure of the pot with magic properties.
15. *Between Men: English Literature and Male Homosocial Desire*, preface to rev. ed. (New York: Columbia University Press, 1992). Sedgwick is a critic I can recommend for both style and insight, whatever one's field of inquiry, even if her specialty, queer readings of literary texts, has nothing to do with one's own research.

work you need them to be doing. Map everything spatially. Finally, though, if your writing is driven by some stubbornly powerful fascination, embrace that obsession. Remember that some of the most valuable books cling to odd shapes and powerful unorthodox messages *because that's what the author's writing needs*. We in turn need those books. We need their challenges and disruptions, and whatever other forms their ideas may take.

I hope I've been able to persuade you that there's never just one way to write or revise. Writers are different from one another, and writers' projects are different, too. But by pausing to reflect on your materials and the questions you're asking of them and with them, the problems you're investigating and the story you're telling about those problems, you've put yourself where you need to be. Now you're really ready to press that start button on your revision. Ready, that is, to go from good to better.

Gnothi seauton, cautioned the ancient Greeks. *Know thyself*. But since that's a heavy lift, at least know thy manuscript. Writing, that thing that looks flat on the page, plays out in multiple dimensions. Which brings us back to three important words beginning with the letter A. Whether you're writing or revising, imagine your work as located along our three axes: *argument, architecture, audience*. Revise with those three in mind. As best you can, make them the objectives of each section, each paragraph, even each sentence you commit to.

Let's look now at the first of those three, the objective that most academic writers think of as their primary obligation: proving something.

4

Look for an argument

"Wait, of course I have an argument! Do I need to *look* for it?"

Although this book is urging you to think about your writing as an act of narrative analysis, there's no getting around the reality that readers of those narrative analyses want to know what's at stake. Arguments are important because they position the writer, crystallizing a stance on some issue the writer wants the reader to take seriously, and because they invite engagement by the reader on that issue. An essay's argument may be subtler than that of a book-length polemic, or the essay might be polemical and the book all detailed needlework, and that's fine. But the difference is usually one of degree, not kind. The argument of any piece of narrative analysis is what should remain with an attentive reader. Argument, examples, anecdotes, delicious writing if you can produce it—you want your reader to come away with all of these, but the first and most important of these is argument.

If you've reread your draft straight through wondering exactly what you had in mind when you started (it all seemed so clear then), you might know what the reader will feel like.

All these ideas! All this information! All those footnotes! True, your reader might jump around and skip the boring bits, for any number of reasons. There are plenty of factors you can't control (a reader's family obligations, work deadlines, energy level). But let's work on the ones that you can.

Most drafts contain wonderful things, and most drafts don't show off those wonders effectively. Some drafts are dull. Some are poorly organized. Some aren't sure who they're written for. Some seem unclear about the distinction between dutiful summary and original insight. Some hope that writing pyrotechnics might dazzle or sheer bulk equate to authority.

Readers want to know what your point is. Readers aren't passive recipients. They're entitled to know the reason you're taking up your words and their time. The shorthand term for that reason is *argument*.

If you're at the revision stage, you should know what your argument is. If you have lingering doubts, this chapter focuses on what arguments are and how they do what they're supposed to do. At the revision stage, this should be a refresher and not a surprise. If you're starting all over again on a new project, though, these pages can help you focus.

First, an *argument* doesn't have to be combative. It's not a swipe or a punch. It's what you have to say. So what are you writing *about*? Anyone who writes will recognize this is the most common question a writer has to face.[1]

When asked, novelists might say something about setting or maybe historical period. ("It's the night before the Battle of Borodino . . .") Nonfiction writers might say something about the materiality of their subject. ("Have you ever thought about why your refrigerator is cold?") Playwrights

---

1. Most common, that is, after the inevitable "So when's it coming out?"

might set up the central conflict. ("There's an old king and he's also got three daughters and—wait for it—he . . .")

But for scholarly writers, the "about" question is really a two-parter. "What are you writing about?" translates into (1) What's your subject? and (2) *What's your take on it?* In revising your project, you need to know the answers for yourself before you need to know it for anyone else.

More: You need to know your argument better than your reader does. A reader can get lost, be distracted, lose faith. Your job is to keep the reader focused. So focused, in fact, that your argument never slips out of view for very long, and that the reader sees your argument as developing, not just being repeated over and over.

Still more: Your *take on a subject* is your *stake in it*. You build an argument because something clicks for you. If there's no click, the most attentive revision isn't going to make what you're writing sit up and speak. Listen for the click.

GETTING TO MORE THAN "ABOUT"

In telling the reader, or yourself, what your argument is, look for specific, delimiting words. Don't settle for generalities. A lot of academics, and the writing they produce, stop at simply indicating *aboutness*. "My book is about economic inequality." That's not an argument.

Much depends, of course, on what idea of "about" we're talking about (sorry) and why. That could mean the context of whatever is being discussed, but it too often means something more like approaching your subject by circling round and round, getting closer and closer without ever getting there. If the imagery of mathematics helps here, you might describe this as a hyperbolic spiral, infinitely turning in ever-tighter circles without meeting its central point.

If your answer to the "about" question is fundamentally descriptive—if your response is essentially a summary of a narrative—you've missed the point of the query. ("It's about the French Revolution and these jewels that go missing. You see, there's this necklace and the sans-culottes are outside with pitchforks and . . .") "What's it *about*?" is shorthand for "Tell me quickly its subject, why that's interesting, and what you have to say about it."[2] Can you do this in a minute or less? You might now recall the last academic conference you attended in real space, and the escalator that goes from the convention hotel lobby down to the book exhibit. Not every hotel escalator conversation has to get to the level of the writer's argument, but an argument there has to be. A narrative, too.

For the writer, the aboutness of a writing project changes over time, even over the time it takes to draft a version of the whole thing. At the beginning, it's reasonable for a writer to say "my project is about the fate of Christian communities in Egypt since the dissolution of the UAR." Six chapters later, the writer knows a lot more, not merely about the fate of Christian communities in Egypt, but also what's interesting about them, and how an argument about them might develop. Sometimes research happens simply because of curiosity and accident. A wall crumbles and an iron box reveals itself. Inside are documents. New information is exposed to air and light. It might take years of study before that new information can provide the basis for a new argument. Not every project begins with an understanding of what's at stake, but time and persistence will lead the writer to ask a

---

2. Sometimes the academic version of this question translates as "What paradigm are you displacing? Whose theory are you exploding? Who are you picking a fight with now?" But it can also translate as "What new thing have you discovered?"

crucial question and form an argument with it. Keep your eye out for iron boxes, which can turn up when you least expect them.

Arguments aren't just provocations. They're windows into how someone goes about questioning. The oldest surviving poem in Old English is a prayer attributed to a cowherd named Caedmon. It's come down to us through the eighth-century *Eccelesiastical History* of the Venerable Bede. Caedmon's hymn praises God, both for his power and for his *modgeþanc* (pronounced something like "mode-ye-thank"). It's my favorite word in the hymn. *Modgeþanc* gets translated as thought, or intention, or mind-plans, or even mood-think. I've wondered if it might also be conveying something like an "idea of a world."

When a scholarly reader, or an academic editor, asks what a piece of writing is about, the question doesn't seek a purely descriptive response. It's curiosity about your purpose and mind-plans. The question is asking about the idea of a world that you've created.

Let's get imaginary for a moment. What if arguments aren't strong, free-standing assertions but instead the principal inhabitants of idea-worlds? I wondered whether this usage was a truism (you can see that this isn't going to be even a shallow dive into metaphysics) and poked around the internet to see what "idea-world" might turn up.

There's *IDEA World* (the all-caps being particularly important), which bills itself as the biggest expo for fitness club managers and entrepreneurs, complete with presentations, networking opportunities, and product launches.

That event is not to be confused with Ideal World, a British entity that bills itself as "the home of TV shopping" and sells all sorts of things you didn't know you were living without, at least so far. Neither of these is to be confused with *Ideen-*

welt. Though that might sound like a Kantian jamboree held on a frigid Baltic seashore, it's really a Viennese expo that focuses on crafting and DIY techniques.[3] Big, ambitious, decidedly corporate ideas, stuff you buy because you get an idea that you need it, stuff you make because you get an idea that you can.

The idea-world of scholarship isn't much like this. It's constructed out of institutions and research sites, institutional housing and, above all, people. But the vital fluid that drives the idea-world is simply the insights and claims that people put forward: theories and arguments that are invented, discovered, or corrected. Knowing what you want to argue, which is knowing what you think and why, isn't only important for you as a writer. It's also essential to building out the idea-world in which scholars continue to think and work and live.

So who is an argument for? Earlier we put forward the concept of the *generative insight*, which now turns out to be an argument that the reader can use. What is the generative insight in your article, the thing that can cause other ideas to happen? Academic writers collect and uncover (facts, artifacts, documents) in the hope of formulating the generative insight. It's the brass ring of scholarship because it makes further, valuable progress possible.

Your idea-world is the set of assumptions you build on and probably disrupt a bit. It's the problem you're investigating, its principal agents, maybe even people, places, and things put into a dynamic relationship through the power of your writing. This idea-world has a subject (the thing you're

3. https://www.ideafit.com/fitness-conferences/idea-world-club-studio-summit; https://www.idealworld.tv/gb/; https://www.ideen-welt.at/de.html. There's even an IDEA World scholarship, which funds attendance at that organization's annual convention.

studying) and a narrative (the track you're making through the subject). What's important at this stage is to be clear about not only your subject but also your narrative, and its position in relation to that subject.

In the kind of writing that practicing academics spend their time producing, "about" doesn't cut it. Knowing what you have is the precondition to knowing what you have to say about it. That in turn is the precondition for formulating a cogent, developable position, the thing for which the term *argument* is really shorthand. In other words, your argument is an idea that's part of and contributes to something bigger than itself.

A good argument is a piece of an ecology of thought. It's not only defensible but also sustainable and productive, and it makes others think in new and different ways. How to develop an argument? Start with what bothers you.

FIRST, A PROBLEM

Here are three categories of problems we all love to spend our time on:

We don't understand it.
We understand it wrong.
We didn't know there was an it.

Or, in less aphoristic terms, we write in order to figure something out, or to correct errors in the way that something has been understood so far, or to *invent* a problem for investigation.

These are such everyday features of writing, especially analytic narrative writing, that we don't stop to think much about them. But we're living in complicated times, and one of the ways in which that complexity shows its face is by mixing up all sorts of categories. New ideas, new problems, new dangers, new causes for hope: for a lot of writers, it's the messiness itself that provides the opportunity to think in fresh ways.

Here's one example. Studying how people become poor rather than how they remain poor might be a way of reframing sets of questions in economics, politics, sociology, and urban studies, with plenty of room for exploring the experience of particular groups of people at particular moments in history. "The Rise of Behavioral Economic Masculinity," an essay by Michelle Chihara, investigates the form in which economic behavior is explained to the lay reader or listener. Its abstract begins with four key sentences:

> This essay begins a cultural history of the behavioral economic narrative mode in American popular media, in relation to the academic discipline but not coincident with it. From podcasts to Michael Lewis's books and films, the behavioral economic mode of narration changes the character or figure of economic knowledge. Instead of the distant financial expert, this mode insists on the authority of the friendly explainer. In the years around the 2008 crisis, at a moment when financial scandals seemed to be losing their power to scandalize, this mode asserted behavioral economic knowledge as the new standard of realism.[4]

By laying out her intention to "begin a cultural history," the author indicates that her problem falls into Problem Category 3: we didn't know there was an it (and now we will learn

4. "The Rise of Behavioral Economic Masculinity," *American Literary History* 32, no. 1 (Spring 2020):77-110, https://academic.oup.com/alh/advance-article/doi/10.1093/alh/ajz055/5688640.

something new). Alternatively, her argument suggests that what we understand concerning the ways in which popular messaging concerning economics works is, or has been, wrong (Problem Category 2).

Sometimes the most valuable questions are the ones that shock us with their newness. Discovering that there is an *it* can be the writer's most valuable contribution. Maybe the *it* is a theoretical concept or object or stage that has been invisible in the past. Or maybe the *it* is a formation or identity or condition that has long been among us but is only now achieving visibility.

Visibility can be literal. Think of an astronomical phenomenon, the description of which is newly possible as a result of technological advances, like the revelations in Galileo's *Starry Messenger*. Or it can be metaphorical, and no less real for that. The *it* might be a new political identity, an explanation for social behavior that has gone unstudied because unremarked, a way of accounting, a way of telling a story. If you stage an argument well, you can persuade the reader that an *it* really does exist and is deserving of study.

Know the kind of problem that's central to your argument.

WHAT ARGUMENTS DO

In academic writing, the argument is often the unique contribution, the central and controlling point, which the writer establishes and defends through the careful use of evidence. Evidence is usually textual or statistical or photographic, though there are other ways of assembling evidence to bolster what one has to say.

So what is an argument, anyway? In its strictest sense, it's a logical proposition. In the pure oxygen breathed by logicians, where "if p then q" can open rich veins of thought about the nature of being, truth, and reality itself, *argument* means one thing. In earlier periods, the *argument* of a play or a long poem might be its situation or its bare-bones plot. In 1668, *Paradise Lost*'s printer, Samuel Simmons, persuaded John Milton to provide "arguments" (abstracts or plot summaries) for each of the poem's books. The poet obliged.

Milton wrote to justify the ways of God to man. Most academics have more modest objectives.

Argument itself has long been a subject of discussion and critique (and, yes, argument). In the field of rhetoric and composition, the nature of argument is no small thing. The British philosopher Stephen Toulmin published his influential *The Uses of Argument* in 1958, a work that resonated both with the field of composition studies and with the emerging field of computer science, one of the connections between the two being that arguments involve logical order.

Order, yes. But is an orderly argument true? Does it have to be? The *Oxford English Dictionary* offers a definition that puts the burden of the question on us. An argument is "a statement of fact offered for the purpose of influencing the mind."[5] That sense of "argument" is traceable in English to the fourteenth century, but its connections to the structure of syllogism links it to the time of Aristotle.

What does that mean for us now? Writing that has "an argument" is doing two things simultaneously. It's stating that something is true and announcing the evidence to persuade you to accept that statement. And yes, its purpose is, as the *OED* makes plain, to influence the mind. Proving your argument through evidence is the first step in influencing the mind, but serious writing aims to do more than that: it

5. Definition 3 (1 being archaic and 2 being astronomical).

wants to change the reader's mind for good, not simply convince the reader that the writer is smart. A novelist may want to persuade you to accept her characters as if they were real, even though both she and you know they aren't. A poet may want to persuade you that words can, despite everything we know about the limits of language, let us in on essential, life-changing half-truths. These aren't arguments, exactly.

Scholarly writing and other forms of ambitious nonfiction have other fish to fry. A scholar knows that an argument is a risk, a tightrope act either with or without a net, and that the stakes are what make the argument possible. You already know what that feels like inside your head:

> *I claim X because I believe X is true. It's not self-evidently, obviously true—a thing that everybody takes for granted—because if it were there wouldn't be any point in my claiming X.*

You wouldn't claim that water is wet, for example.[6]

> *Since X is not obviously true—at least to you, at least yet—I am going to parcel out a series of explanatory events to convince you of X. If it weren't necessary to produce this series, I wouldn't have had a claim to begin with.*

But in writing, the formula argument + evidence isn't just about logical proof, and here is where the logical-mathematical model has to give way to reveal the social and human dimension that makes writing worth the trouble.

The writer needs the risk of being unconvincing in order

6. Many published articles and even book-length studies nonetheless fall into the "water is wet, and I'll prove it" category of argumentation. You've probably read some.

to produce a series of events (data sets, historical documents, fieldwork observations, close textual readings) that stand as corroborations. Each of those corroborating events is a kind of story built from facts that are then interpreted by the writer and summoned in support of the argument. Or, to put it another way, the risk makes the evidence possible as evidence.

We can take this one step further. Scholarly nonfiction at its best describes something incompletely, or incorrectly, understood about the world. That description involves making a claim—which means saying something at least a little bit new, and at least a little bit surprising—in order to "influence the mind" of the reader. Influence how? To persuade or dissuade, to unsettle or assure, to incite or calm, or any of the many other ways in which attentive readers might respond to attentive writers. At the same time, the particular risk entailed in making a claim becomes the writer's opportunity to share stories (data sets, historical documents, fieldwork observations, close textual readings) that might otherwise not be told, or shared, or analyzed. Or read, or debated, or enjoyed, or fought over.

To "influence the mind" isn't anything like persuading the reader that vanilla ice cream is better than chocolate. (Some days yes, some days no, if you ask me.) For a writer, persuading a reader of the writer's claim is the cumulative effect of all those presentations of evidence, all those delivered events, made of words, each of which takes its own risks, each of which proposes to describe something about the world, choosing word after word, and with each choice a decision, which becomes a little risk in itself.

That's a bit vertiginous as a description of how argumentative writing works, but if you're revising to make things merely clearer, if you're revising without a sense of how ter-rifically dangerous writing is, and you're still not aiming to change your reader's mind, you're missing out on what argu-ment is capable of. Besides, you're depriving yourself of the risk, which is the fun of putting words and ideas down, one after another, and watching them do their work. For writers, argument and narrative are twinned. Good writing is driven by narrative, and good academic writers do more than de-scribe and explain, page by page.

If you're a scholarly writer, you have a professional obli-gation to the history of thought about your subject and to re-sponsibly presenting that history as part of your own original ideas. That points to a tension at the heart of argument-driven writing. The *argument itself*, the big thing you're trying hard to say, has to be summarizable, while at the same time the *writing itself* is extensive, sometimes book-length, in order to prove the argument and let it speak.

Quantitative analyses compress argument (and, we might suggest, narrative) in the service of crisp, mathematically derived evidence presented as clearly as possible. In quanti-tative analysis, the priority is placed on the values of objec-tivity and neutrality, concepts that qualitative analysis also pursues, if perhaps with a bit more skepticism. But even the article that groans under the weight of tables and charts and is light on declarative sentences will have ordered its ele-ments so as to take the reader through an argument. Qualita-tive analyses, which by definition argue from different ideas of evidence, depend more heavily on language, and with language comes a different order of complexity and possi-bility. Each mode searches for truth, though method itself may have a hand in determining what truth or argument will look like.

The phrase "to make an argument" might be a way of thinking about the double responsibility of positioning an idea briefly ("the argument") and the exposition of that brief positioning over the course of whatever you're writing. Think of the argument, then, in two perspectives: the pithy thing you can say in an interview and the time-consuming, detail-driven narrative in which you place and nurture it. Looked at that way, your text is making the argument, page by page, chapter by chapter. It's a way of thinking about writing that refuses a simple, and often stagnant, architecture, with argument up front and supporting examples following on, chapter by chapter. To put it still another way, persuasive writing is suffused by its argument. If that makes your writing a little messy, a little uncontrolled, that's fine.

Academic argument is elaborated over time. When done well, it's rich with events and examples, built on the history of ideas, practices, theories, and interventions, components brought to the fore to be ordered and properly acknowledged, all so that the writer can propose a carefully presented idea and make it stick. Argument, then, is more like narrative than we may want to acknowledge.

PINPOINT AN IDEA

Where does an argument begin? The legal profession demonstrates that arguments are made in responses to disputes. Cases emerge when parties cannot agree, and so a problem is formulated. From that problem, arguments are made. Thinking about writing shares this with the procedure of the legal brief: the motivation to craft an argument emerges from the recognition of a problem.

If a scholar is going to argue something that no one cares about or on which everyone already agrees, then there's no reason for crafting the argument in the first place. For example, no one would simply argue that chattel slavery is a bad thing, because everyone surely agrees that chattel slavery is a bad thing. What one might argue, facing the grim realities of twenty-first-century global life, is that conditions of servitude for which the term "slavery" is not generally applied are, in fact, precisely that and not to be dimmed through appeals to tradition or family autonomy or the systematic dispensation of minimal compensation. For scholars, arguments emerge from looking conditions squarely in the eye and seeing that something is inaccurate, incomplete, misunderstood. Why bother to make an argument that something we all abhor is terrible and stop there?

If you're crafting an argument, you're looking for trouble. Finding it may not be a happy thing, but it's a good thing. Good, because now you're able to articulate for yourself the gap, the error, that you will seek to fill in or correct. Filling in and correcting may sound like a dull summary of a lifetime of scholarly work, but it will only look that way to non-scholars. And of course, once in a while a scholar is able to make an argument that changes everything.

I sometimes work with groups of scholars on their writing projects. We focus on getting them to name what they're writing about and what they have to say. The Writing Bullseye is an exercise you might use for developing large-scale writing projects. The Writing Bullseye has clear but not so simple goals. In search of the aboutness of a project, the exercise sets up limits within which to say what you think your writing project takes as its objective. Think of the exercise as stages on the way to an argument.

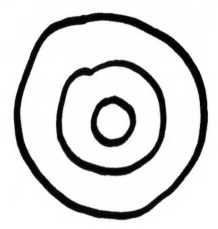

4.1 The Writing Bullseye.

The Writing Bullseye certainly looks simple enough. A diagram: three concentric rings (figure 4.1).

First, the outer ring. Here you name the object of your project. At the most basic level, this is where you locate its "aboutness" (remember: *aboutness* is not a goal in itself, much less an argument). If you're working in a group, the person leading the exercise might give the group these directions:

1. Describe your project using no more than ten words. (No cheating). Do *not* create a sentence, i.e., do not connect a subject grammatically to a predicate.

The goal is to postpone saying definitively why you're writing what you're writing about.

Some examples, from three writers working on the history of American horticulture, environmental pollution in southeast Asia, and police violence:

The introduction of non-native insects in mid-twentieth-century North America.

The toxicity of airborne particulate matter in modern-day Bangkok.

Public cynicism and perceptions of police brutality.

Next, the middle ring. Here you name an existing problem that emerges from the object. This is that something within your subject that catches your eye.

2. Phrase in the form of a declarative sentence the problem you are writing about. In the second ring, our three scholars write:

In an effort to limit the expansion of introduced insect pests, researchers travel to these insects' native environments to better understand how their natural enemies might be used to control them, though at the risk of introducing further pest species.

Governmental efforts to control air pollution in Bangkok have failed.

A recent study, analyzing the frequency of 911 calls after a 2005 incident, has a design flaw.[7]

Writing out the problem is an opportunity to ask yourself whether you've got close enough in, and whether the

7. I'm drawing on these sources but simplifying for the purposes of this exercise. See US Forestry Service, "Invasive Species," https://www.fs.fed.us/research/invasive-species; BBC World News, "Bangkok schools closed over 'unhealthy' level of pollution," January 30, 2019, https://www.bbc.com/news/world-asia-pacific-47057128; Michael Zoorob, "Do Police Brutality Stories Reduce 911 Calls? Reassessing an Important Criminological Finding," *American Sociological Review* 85, no. 1 (February 2020): 176–83, https://journals.sagepub.com/doi/10.1177/0003122419895254.

problem as you've stated it provides an adequate platform for your thinking. Can you drill down from this? Will the problem, as you've named it, help you shape your ideas? Is it the "good kind of problem"?

Finally, the innermost circle.

3. What question are you asking about the problem you've identified? For this part of the exercise, your response should be framed as an interrogative.

> What has the experience of the Florida ecosystem taught us about introducing biological deterrents to control invasive species?

> How does the discourse of environmental pollution distribute responsibility between Bangkok's industries, Thai agriculture, and individual urban residents?

> If we correct for a design flaw, what conclusions about public cynicism and police brutality can this data set show us?

The heart of a scholarly argument might be thought of as *the question you ask about a problem you perceive*. The problem will exist either in your object of study or in the state of our knowledge of that object of study. So your note to self might resemble this:

> I'm interested in Subject S, and I'm interested in particular because of Problem P. There's no sign that Problem P is going to go away by itself, or that we're on track to understand it any better than we currently do. So I'm writing what I'm writing to ask a question—Ask1—about the problem. That's going to make Problem P more difficult, at least at

first, and will probably move me on to Ask2 and Ask3, but it's a place where I think I can make a useful intervention concerning the state of Subject S.

You might be saying that these concentric circles only point you to what you're writing about, and not your argument. But that misunderstands the nature of argument, especially the sort of arguments that scholars develop and sustain.

If you're developing a scholarly idea, it has to be clearly and persuasively presented first to other scholars, whose approval is going to validate it. After that, the scholarly idea may have further destinations and appear in alternate forms—as a white paper, an op-ed, an essay for a general interest magazine. Ideas aren't confined to one level of complexity. An idea that takes off will have a life of its own.

TEST FOR COUNTERFACTUALITY

Revision is a chance to think backward, or maybe athwart (nice word) your idea. Of course, you believe in your argument. If it's a good one, it should invite criticism. Testing for counterfactuality is taking an idea and turning it around to get a better view. It's stopping to listen to your argument from a different perspective. You're working with premises, theories, and data that have to be interpreted to have meaning, and so you have to build into that interpretation certain assumptions.

Some forms of writing take on a juridical tone and line up the pros and cons before reaching a conclusion.

"Here are the reasons why summer breaks should be six weeks and no longer." "Nonsense! Here are the reasons why students need three months off."

Pros and cons need to be sufficiently complete so that the reader isn't leaping up to cry, "But what about . . . ?" Few forms of writing will stage an argument quite so schematically. More often, the writer needs to listen to what is being argued and consider where weaknesses may lie.

Sometimes it's best to present a counterargument directly, bringing it to light so that it can be demolished. "Because Shakespeare doesn't extend the final scene of *The Winter's Tale*, we don't know what will happen to Hermione and Leontes. There are those who see the couple as reconciled, since the play does not explicitly say otherwise. I argue here that the play's silences confirm the impossibility of repairing the marriage."

Incorporating the "other view" into one's writing makes what you have to say more persuasive, and while it may take a few more words to bring in another view, the overall effect is the impression of greater economy: more muscle and less fat. As you revise, test your ideas. Ask: "What if I'm wrong? What if my assumption is unsubstantiated?" If you're a scholar, you're trained to produce yards of evidence upon request, but it's still possible, even necessary, to make assumptions. That means it's still possible to go off on the wrong track. If you didn't need to make at least some assumptions, would there be a problem left worth exploring?

Counterarguments either propose an opposing view to your claim or destabilize your claim by attempting to neutralize your working premises or your factual assertions:

> There are no contaminants. And if there are, their level isn't rising. And if they're rising, they're not rising sufficiently to account for the change in the speckled trout population.

Or:

You've read the scientific reports, but you've read them incorrectly. And even if you've read the reports correctly, you're working with bad reports, since the sampling is too small to provide data upon which larger conclusions can be built.

Or:

What you say about contaminants may or may not be true, but there is another factor that you have failed to consider, and that is the diversion of water to the swamps.

Consider this an opportunity to think about what views contrary to your own claims might sound like, and what they might mean for someone interested in the subject. (Be assured that if you publish a big claim that runs counter to an established view, your argumentation and evidence will be subject to scrutiny.) Any form of writing that involves research will involve an appeal to the expertise of other authorities, experts, observers, and archives. Remember that footnotes are there for you to document the care with which you've undertaken your research, not a place to hide important parts of your argument, much less to substitute for an argument that you haven't yet made.

Footnotes are supports and authentications, but they're there to support and authenticate something bigger, something important you want to tell your reader. (And occasionally for asides.)

When you revise, you take a moment to step back. A big moment, a big step. What does whatever you're writing claim? How does that claim differ from what has been asserted by others? To your readers, your claim is a kind of news. You're offering something fresh and up-to-date on your chosen subject. But it's also useful to think about your authorities, those powerful figures in your footnotes and bibliography. "If authority X were to read what I have to say today, would X's view change?" "Could I persuade someone who I acknowledge to be one of the important figures in my discipline?"

The objective of nonfiction writing is to make a claim about the world. A claim is only worth paying attention to if it is (a) backed up with persuasive argument and evidence, and (b) sufficiently different from what the reader already assumes to warrant attention in the first place. So the claim is an act of argument and persuasion. It's what makes writing dynamic. The claim says that something is true. That true something might be a genuine discovery, or if not quite a discovery then at least a fresh insight. Or working backward, your true something might be the revelation that what we've assumed to be true isn't true at all. Or it might be something in between. Maybe an adjustment to what we have thought, but an adjustment in light of new facts or theories. A discovery, a reversal, an adjustment: a claim can be any or all of these things.

Now prove it. When we pose that challenge to a student, a colleague, the book we're reading, or to ourselves, we're asking that a claim be strengthened. Some writers discuss the argument in purely logical terms: assemble your data, line up your arguments, display your evidence, be sure everything is in order, and press Enter. This sort of regimentation has its place, though more in scientific calculations than in narrative-based analyses of human experience. Working through argument and evidence, you might even find yourself feeling a bit nostalgic for the rigorous simplicity of Euclidean geometry in the schoolrooms of your youth.

You're probably not working on calculating the area of a rhomboid just now. Language is at least as complicated as geometry, or so it seems to this non-mathematician. In any case, there are few circumstances where you will find yourself writing anything longer than a single page and not encountering the many ways in which language wiggles out of geometry's stern but comforting rules for proving a point (or angle). Language can't prove the way Euclid proved, but language does other things. Watch out for category mistakes.

Before signing off on your claim, give it a 360-degree once-over. There's more than one way to skin a cat (though it's less than clear why anyone would want to).

GETTING TO PROOF

When we ask for proof from a writer, we want to be convinced that what the writing is saying is well-grounded and effectively argued. Rarely are we willing to accept the writer's claims without organized and persuasive argument. If you're a Red Sox fan, you might need little argumentative persuasion to agree with the columnist who leads off with the assertion that the Sox are really much more interesting than the Yankees and, over the next five years, will demonstrate that they are the greatest baseball team in America. But your assent as a Red Sox fan is at least partly emotional, not rational. It would be just the same if you were a Yankees fan reading a journalist touting the Yankees. The columnist you instantly agree with might be said to be preaching to the choir, asserting a proposition to an audience that accepts it on faith.

Argument isn't like that, though it would be possible to develop a set of criteria by which one argued that one team is more interesting than another, a discrimination that could incorporate stats but not rely exclusively on them. The marriage of data and interpretation, fact and something more human-based, might in this case yield a rich and ongoing argument about sports teams and the reasons to follow them.

Of course, some arguments aren't arguments at all. They may be exercises in slicing thin things even more thinly. Or present old news as new (a publishing wag once remarked about especially lifeless manuscripts that they "broke old ground"). Ted Underwood alerts readers to a subtler problem:

> I am wary of the academic tendency to simultaneously disavow and appropriate the past by rebranding it. ("Everyone knows that distant reading was naïve, but I have invented *critical* distance reading, which is quite another matter!") Endless rebranding is tiresome.[8]

Argument—and writing in general—fails when it's perceived as weak. If you're reading your revision and sensing that the argument is weak, think about three possible deficits:

Deficit One. The claim isn't really a claim at all, just a restatement of what we have believed using different examples.

Deficit Two. Historic and critical innocence. Do your homework. Not just in bibliographic terms but also with sensitivity to the history—the histories, all of which may not agree with one another—of your subject. History, both diachronic and synchronic, is inescapably important evidence. Use both.

---

8. Preface to *Distant Horizons: Digital Evidence and Literary Change* (Chicago: University of Chicago Press, 2019).

Deficit Three. Making a claim that isn't backed up respon-
sibly. A more explicit version of Deficit Two. (Do your
homework.) If you don't, you will be called out. Read other
people's work on your subject. That's evidence, too.

Don't be afraid of data, but remember that it requires interpretation, and that means it bears the burden of narrative.
Observable data (I'm shifting to the plural now) are not in
themselves facts, unless we understand a fact as something
made (the word comes from the Latin *factum*). Made things
need explaining.

Facts require interpretation. Data, like the creatures in
the natural world, need us to say for them what they cannot
say for themselves. And when we give voice to data, or
facts, or animals, it's our job to get as close as possible to
the reality demonstrated by those nonhuman, nonspeaking
phenomena and fellow worldlings and to the signs by which
we understand them.

What do the data tell us? And what do we say back to them?
The narratives we make from data and facts aren't necessarily good (or bad), but once we recognize the madeness
of narrative, and of the things on which narrative depends,
we're able to see that the world around us is constantly subject to and in need of interpretation. That's good, if not uncomplicated, news. It's what occupies scholars, critics, and
attentive observers of all stripes.

Don't be afraid of world and life experience, including oral
history. A lot of what we have failed to see around us might
provide the key to understanding our own failures and weaknesses, even as we set about the task of making some aspect
of the world a better, and better understood, place. Give
voice to the voiceless. That's one of the writer's jobs, especially if the writer is a scholar.

So have we got any closer to what argument is and what it does? We've pressed the point that an argument is a form of narrative about ideas. Or, alternatively, narrative is a form of argument about the world. The distinguished economist Robert Shiller is another specialist who has been able to write for a general audience. In *Narrative Economics: How Stories Go Viral and Drive Major Economic Events* he focuses on the narrative component of data, those "contagious popular stories that spread through word of mouth, the news media, and social media." He proposes that a methodology of *narrative* economics "can improve our ability to anticipate and prepare for economic events. It can also help us structure economic institutions and policy."[9] If Shiller urges us to consider the utility of narrative, we'd better listen.

Good argument balances accuracy (thinking big, thinking fairly) with precision (thinking small, thinking surgically). In revising, work hard not to be partial. When we say that someone's view is *partial* we mean that it's biased or demonstrates a preference. "Sally's choice of hapkido over aikido showed that she was partial to aggressive martial arts. Nobody who knew Sally would have been surprised."

But *partial* also means incomplete or selective. "Jesse's partial explanation for the fender bender left out an important detail. Yes, the road was rough and the other car had a light missing, but Jesse had also downed three cans of Red Bull since breakfast."

You want your writing to be not partial but impartial, not partial but complete. Tell your story as fully as you can and be sure that all the context and surrounding argument is presented to the reader. That way, what you yourself add,

---

9. *Narrative Economics: How Stories Go Viral and Drive Major Economic Events* (Princeton, NJ: Princeton University Press, 2019), 1.

delete, substitute, or correct will make much more sense. Besides, when you convincingly commit to being accurate, your reader trusts you. The reader needs to trust the writer to be fair, truthful, and as complete as possible, which is why this chapter about the centrality of argument to successful revision makes what look like detours into pretty simple rules of the road.

To argue well, listen well. That's fundamentally the work of analysis as we understand it, and it's the foundational premise of scholarship. Pay attention to what does and doesn't happen.[10] To do that, and to do that well, we use narrative and shape from it a premise we call argument.

When you're revising your writing, you're listening to your facts and your data to see if you've given them voice.[11] And to make sure that when you've allowed them to speak, you listen. That listening may be the researcher's most precious skill: the ornithologist parsing a rare bird's vocalizations, the anthropologist permitted to observe the sounds and sights of a burial ritual, the Arctic specialist attuned to the variety of sounds a calving glacier makes. A writer is like none of these and all of them, listening for elements and details generated in many different ways.

What one sees and hears, though, has to be shown to be shared. The goal of writing isn't to entomb one's knowledge or lock away one's insight for safekeeping. You write for two reasons and two reasons only: first, to find out what you think, and, second, to share what you think with others.

10. In Conan Doyle's story "The Adventure of Silver Blaze," Sherlock Holmes cracks the case because a dog does *not* bark during a nighttime incident. Good writing listens for what is there, what isn't there, what might be expected not to be there (but is), what might be expected to be there (and isn't).
11. We can make here a connection between the work of anthropology and other forms of disciplinary listening.

Sharing what you think doesn't happen automatically. It's an outcome you the writer work to produce. You do that work by being persuasive, mustering argument, crafting a structure that supports your argument, gently moving the reader forward. You do something more, too: by giving your reader tools or, as we might think of them in even more immediate terms, *takeaways*.

TAKEAWAYS

A conclusion is a takeaway, and an important one if you've constructed a tight and artful thesis. There are other kinds of takeaways, too, and no writer wants to overlook them. Think small so your reader can think big: specific, exportable, usable consequences of your writing will be gratefully embraced, struggled over, built upon by your readers.

Here are three takeaways beyond conclusion.

Memorable example. Some kinds of writing revel in the anecdote and the symptomatic case (though a case *study* is usually too long to be memorable). You choose an incident or application as an example in order to bolster your argument. Something strong, something succinct, and if it's memorable—delightful or harrowing or otherwise unforgettable—even better. Crafty writers plan, plant, and leverage the memorable example. Revision is a chance to be crafty.

Linguistic tool. Sometimes what the reader takes away is a turn of phrase, a neologism, an updating of a familiar expression made suddenly powerful because newly vigorous. Secret writing tip: choose something you want to highlight— a concept you can convey in a phrase—and bring it forward so the reader knows you want it to stick. Like the other arts, writing deploys the distinction of figure and ground, as well as the inevitable power of repetition. Figure out what figure you want to emphasize and make it a takeaway for your reader. Say what's important at least twice. Then repeat it, but not in exactly the same words.

Application. Most studies will argue that something can be explained by something else, and explained in a new way. If you're writing that kind of book, you might be able to show the reader some tools for exploring the world beyond your book and its analytic project. Books are memorable for the pleasure they give, the windows they open, and the new tools they offer. Giving the reader a theory and a little push to apply it is a complex takeaway, but it might be the one that makes the most lasting impression.

An argument is much more than concisely worded tough talk. It's an idea with an ambition to change things. For that to take place effectively on the page, your text has to settle on the right shape for presenting the idea. That's where architecture comes in.

5

Build an architecture

Writer, concept architect, space-wrangler: go ahead and put all three professional credits on an imaginary version of your CV. Writing is words arranged in shapes, and part of revising is making the right shape for the kind of writing you're strengthening.

It can always be helpful to look at the way fields unlike your own think about terms that seem important to what you're doing. In the discipline of computer engineering, for example, the sets of rules that govern a system can be referred to as a computer's architecture. When you have more than one, you speak of computer *architectures*.[1]

Of course, there are the lyric poets, who hear better than most of us. Keats and Auden call forth "architectured" landscapes, observing nature giving itself shape, as well as what humans do *to* nature.[2] Be prepared to architecture your ideas.

---

1. See, for example, John L. Hennessy and David A. Patterson, *Computer Architecture: A Quantitative Approach*, 6th ed. (Cambridge, MA: Elsevier, 2019), 2.
2. Keats marvels at an island cave "architectured thus / By the great Oceanus!" Auden, in *Journey to a War*, describes a slope, viewed from

Academics write complicated work that develops in complicated ways and sometimes requires complicated architectures. So does fiction (modernism, anyone?). "Only connect," the famous epigraph to E. M. Forster's 1910 novel *Howards End*, is suggestive and urgent, an injunction that analyzes a problem and impels a solution. Of course, you will say, since making connections between people, classes, ways of thinking, and bolts of prose is obviously a good thing.[3] The question is how to do it.

If you write, you structure. Sometimes you're writing a lean-to, easily disposed of when you break camp. Sometimes you'll write a one-room cabin (maybe something unbearably lovely in a Norwegian wood). Sometimes a multiroom dwelling with public and private spaces of different sizes and purposes. Some projects are commissions, some are dream houses, some are meant to exist only on paper.

They're all what my architect friends seem to mean when they talk about "built environments," the way that structures derive their purpose in part from being integrated into the space and lives in which and for which they're intended.

But what's structure? If we're talking about a building, structure is what keeps the thing up and gives it shape. There isn't much question about what structure means. That's the roof, the hallway, the flying buttress. Beneath, under, above, and within, you'll find building materials and surfacing elements. Beams, girders, stone, concrete. Doors, windows,

---

a train, "architectured into terraces, upon which wheat is growing." *OED*, s.v. "architecture, *v.*"

3. Even if that may not be exactly what Forster intended. See Adam Kirsch's essay "The Prose and the Passion" (*New Republic*, July 13, 2010), which argues that the closeted Forster was marking "the difficulty of connecting our ordinary, conventional personalities with our transgressive erotic desires."

skylights. There are sometimes surprises (I love the way architects talk of the "reveal"), but they're all planned, all in the structure. Of course, sentences aren't rebars or loadbearing walls, and nobody gets hurt if a paragraph collapses. But let's pursue the architectural metaphor to see if it might help us understand what can happen on the page.

In writing, there's the structure you the writer think you've built, and then there's the apparent structure, which is the reader's perception of visible organization within the text.

Perception is *visible* organization. Because whatever the writer may write or intend, it's the reader's perception that drives the reading. Texts can only lay out the words for us. Readers make texts come alive. Readers perceive structure. Readers make texts texts.

Much of what concerns us in thinking about revising prose, then, is the way the reader perceives what the writer may or may not have done. A writer may think that the writing is clearly structured, well paced, and handsomely organized, but it's only when text meets reader that the question takes on a practical reality.

Most writers, including academic ones, write in genres. Genres are disciplinary forms with construction rules. Those rules determine what you say, how you say it, and the shape in which you deliver your ideas. An article in a medical journal on non-small cancers will look different from a sociological study of how physicians talk to children with cancer. Data and narrative may be actively present in both, but they will be weighted differently, occupy space differently, and be used differently by their intended readers. Genres have architecture.

So writing is words, but writing is also shape and space if only we think of it that way—voids and walls, doors and corridors, basements and rooftops. Try thinking of the thing you're revising as a structure that just happens to be made out of language. What structure works best for what you're writing? This may not feel like what you tell yourself you're doing when you write, but when you're deep inside a chapter, or a paragraph, or sometimes even a single sentence, you're comprehending—and weighing the pros and cons of—alternative architectures. You're looking at possibilities, supporting parts, a syntax of information delivery, the conventions of your discipline regarding how things are supposed to be said and in what order.

If that feels too abstract, try thinking about the architecture of the space you inhabit. That on-campus faculty apartment, a brownstone, an entire suburban split-level, or just half a room. You might know the space in terms of its weaknesses (noise, light, leaks) or its proximities (to campus, friends, therapist). Where you live is where you're sheltered, and it's where you shelter a lot of your research materials, too. Housing counts.

In the 1950s, the philosopher Gaston Bachelard composed *The Poetics of Space,* urging the reader to think of ordinary interiors as geometries with profound connections to their setting.[4] We all think about our dwellings, and in different ways. In an interview with *Architectural Digest,* Maya Angelou spoke about her marriage (to a man who happened to be an architect). The marriage worked until it didn't. Angelou told the magazine:

> With all heartsore lovers I say, "I don't know what went wrong." But I suspect it was the house. The living room was two stories high, and I put my large three-by-five-foot paint-

---

4. *The Poetics of Space,* trans. Maria Jolas (Boston: Beacon Press, 1994).

ings on the walls, and my paintings looked like enlarged postage stamps.[5]

There was more, but this is Angelou's way into the subject of love and loss, space and scale.

What house have you built for your ideas? Out of your ideas? A writer examines the pieces and tries to understand how they work, especially when they don't.

In writing, architecture doesn't just present and shelter your thoughts. It persuades. You might not think of architecture as something that needs to be persuasive. Useful, sturdy, yes, even beautiful. Snazzy, theoretically up-to-the-minute, maybe. But persuasive?[6]

Well-structured writing is persuasive writing. Persuasion isn't something that's added to a draft's otherwise unpersuasive architecture, like a paint job over bad walls, either. Persuasiveness emerges *from* argument and evidence, *from* voice and tone, and *from* the piece's architecture.

As you revise, give yourself some simple rules. Aim to have one good, big, important idea in your essay or article or chapter. Just one. If you think of a chapter as a room for that one good idea, you'll be able to move through your revision with a sense of purpose. Don't crowd the wall, no matter how many paintings you have. Remember: this is a wall for others to see, not just a private museum. Work to make everything you add to, or subtract from, your chapter throw more light on your one good, important idea.

Sentences and paragraphs are your building units. You ar-

---

5. "Celebrity Style: "AD revisits Maya Angelou," *Architectural Digest* (May 1, 1994), https://www.architecturaldigest.com/story/maya-angelou -home-essay-article.
6. Architects do, of course. A good structure is responsive, responsible, at one with a site and the community that will use it. The well-built thing is a thing that argues for itself.

range them in order to construct the room of the chapter in the house of the book. The architecture of writing isn't simply a matter of "themes" that run throughout a text; it's the attentive placement of elements so that the walls stand and the reader feels secure.

But there's more to the architecture of writing. It's not just the sturdy, clearly delineated components arranged for immediate comprehension. There's also the rhythm created by the movement of prose, the alternations of length and color, of stern brevity and luxurious indulgence, the ripple of sentences that have been crafted with a feeling for the pulse of language. Architecture isn't just a built environment. Writing isn't just words. Think of either as the persuasiveness of structure and the durability of form in relation to the ideas that animate it.

When you sit down to revise something you've written, the goal of making connections is an architectural problem for which you've given yourself a second chance at the right answer. You'll want to see the parts as if they weren't yours, the ideas moving on the page (or not) as if they weren't already fully under your control. In a sense, you need to disconnect (yourself from your writing so that you can see it clearly) in order to connect (its parts to one another, the whole to your reader). We're back to that writerly veil of ignorance we looked at earlier: making decisions about reading as if you did not—and could not—know, who the reader was.

Writing rule: Work to bring the parts together.

Writing rule with an architectural twist: As you revise, work to bring outlying paragraphs and ideas into the mainstream of your argument. You want to build a structure, not a settlement.

QUESTIONS A WRITER-ARCHITECT ASKS

Despite your designs and structural arrangements, despite your conviction that the argument is solid and a fresh take as well, you will have doubts. That's not only a professional hazard; it's a professional necessity. Don't trust a writer who never has doubts.

Ask yourself questions about the shape of your text. Remember that the architecture of the thing you're writing has to do work. You're building a practical structure.

Why does my text have the shape it does? You've made decisions to deliver information to your reader within the limitations of a particular arrangement. A number of chapters in a certain order. A series of questions from which an argument can be clearly deduced. Tell yourself why you made these choices. Now take a look to see if what's on your page corresponds to what you say you've done.

What happens on page 1 and why? There's nothing more important than your first page. It's not necessarily where the big idea is going to be announced, but if you don't get the first page right, you may lose your reader. Know what you need to set up on page 1: history? theory? a situating moment? a refutation? even a strategic misdirection?

Where is the crucial thought most clearly expressed? This is a trick question, since the crucial thought may be the argument, or it may be a consistently articulated perspective on your subject, something that requires underscoring again and again because that's the kind of thing you're writing. Most of what we do requires that important points be made clearly available to the reader. Remember the concept of narrative analysis we looked at when we began this adventure. You have lots of options, but you've got to make it possible for your reader to recognize your most important takeaway.

Weak architecture is all detail; strong architecture has a focus.

What kinds of signposts do I need? Do I have them where I need them? The kind of writing you're doing determines the tenor of your signposting. The paratexts of an article in a medical journal will be clinically specific. Readers of textbooks will anticipate clear, descriptive, and uncomplicated signage. Humanities specialists, whether writing for their peers or for a general readership, often generate signage that is "voiced," by which they mean it's marked with a feeling of personal presence or opinion. Social scientists often occupy a middle ground between using clinically descriptive markers and "voiced" signage.

Am I putting my lexicon to work? Take another look at your key terms. They're the lexicon that animates what you're writing. Now do a global search of your document to see where they occur. If, for example, the word *agency* is a key term and you discover that it shows up fourteen times in the first half of your text and not at all in the second half, there's probably something missing in the way you're using it. A key term doesn't have to recur again and again (fourteen is a lot), but if it does, it needs to be part of the music of your prose, recurring like a theme or a chord. It's hard to imagine a great song in which the most important chord sequence occurs several times in the first half and then disappears. Can you distribute the occurrences of your key terms so that your reader keeps them in mind all along? If so, you might also be convincing your reader that you've been keeping these terms in mind all along.

Is the length right? Structural issues are always about length. For academic types, the challenge is not to drown the reader while providing the rich detail and analysis that got you into writing this thing to begin with. Coco Chanel advised that before she leaves the house, the well-dressed woman stops, looks in the mirror, and takes off one unnecessary thing. A pin, a bracelet, a string of pearls. Maybe grandmama's tiara. Chanel was living in a moment when to be well dressed evidently meant to have lots of jewelry and such; her concern was that one not be overdressed. It's difficult to think of Chanel's advice as relevant to our largely jewelry-free era, but if (and only if, as the logicians say) you could cut a sentence from a page, a paragraph from a chapter, a chapter from a book-length manuscript, how would you do it? Would it make your text better? If it would, then leave that sentence or paragraph, or even an entire chapter, at the door. Chanel wasn't suggesting you throw your sparklers away, just that you save them for another event. Ditto for the stuff you leave out in your last pass through your revision. Save the scraps, the odd excurses, the extra string of pearly examples.

Could someone other than me summarize what I wrote? You began your revision thinking hard about what you had. When you've completed your revision, it's time to step back and ask yourself once again some of the same questions. What's it about? What's the writer's point? Of course, these are questions you have to be able to answer, but in checking the architecture of your revision aim to imagine how a reader would answer. Pretending to be someone other than yourself is a constant obligation of revision (and a constant theme of the book you're reading). Take up a highlighter, either physically or digitally, and mark what feels most important as you think your reader will. You may discover that there's a missing transition or bit of signposting. The crucial isn't always obvious.

What about the units? Are the sections of your text similar in length? If not, is there a good reason why? What is that good reason, exactly?

And the paragraphs? It doesn't help the reader much if your paragraphs are all the same length and all a page and a half long. Academic writers typically overstuff their writing. One of the easiest and most gratifying ways to improve academic prose is to break paragraphs. It's not hard. Try it.

If you find yourself resisting, try to think purely in terms of visual fatigue. Academic writers can seem nervous about the single-sentence, much less the single-word, paragraph, and they shouldn't. The technique offers the reader a bit of visual and cognitive relief from the long and complicated thinking at which we excel.

It's easy to induce visual fatigue in your reader. Visual relief, on the other hand, can come to the page in several ways, not only through paragraph breaks but also by means of graphic materials, from photographs and sketches to maps, charts, and diagrams. Introducing visual elements into a text is extra work for everyone involved, and some visual elements make the text more rather than less complex. The eye wants a break from an endless series of almost-full-page paragraphs, and even a difficult diagram offers a certain kind of pause. But it's the prose itself where you can most easily provide visual relief, mainly because, unless you're a poet or playwright, or working on a visual project, your text is going to be mostly prose. Big blocks of it.

Try chopping in half any paragraph that fills two-thirds of a page. To do that, you'll need to find a moment in the paragraph that shifts something, that moves the searchlight a few degrees. When you find that moment, press Return. Make a new paragraph. Read it all out loud. You should hear that fulcrum moment with a new emphasis, a new clarity. If you're not hearing the emphasis you want, rewrite the whole page.

You're hardly ever weakening your writing by making two paragraphs from one. You're making an idea clearer and easier for the reader to take in. A new paragraph might be barely a pause in the reader's consciousness, no more dramatic than a new breath. But no new breath, no life. That's a rule both for your reader and your text. Err on the side of breathing.

Yes, yes, but have I got the ending right? Endings are nuanced recaps, summaries, deflections, a place to settle down and bring the performance to a rest, a tool, a box of possibilities, an affirmation, a mystery. The kind of ending you need depends on the kind of thing you're writing and for whom. We'll look at endings again at the end of this book.

SHOW ME

"Show me *now*," sings Eliza Doolittle to the moony-eyed, frustratingly ineffective Freddy Eynsford-Hill in the Lerner and Loewe classic *My Fair Lady*. Writers need to show what they're thinking. Frankly, they hardly have a choice, except to show badly or well. The more visible your structures, the more visible your analytic thinking becomes, the more intentional, the more deliberate.

Can you remember your plans for the first version of the piece you're revising? At the start of it all, you began with some ideas you wanted to show, and you probably had some inkling of limit and shape. If you kept notes, pull them out now. If you have them stored only in memory, write them down. They might have begun with the words, "This summer I intend to write . . ." Or better still, "This summer I'll be revising . . ." What was that again? Your work in progress might be chapter 4 of a dissertation on Asian-Americans and sports management; a six-thousand-word essay for the *Oxford Companion to Disaster Response*; a fourteen-thousand-word review essay on the year's work in arbitration scholarship for *Legal Briefs at Length*; a thirty-five-page chapter for a book on revising writing. Each of these projects started somewhere.

When you began your draft, what shape did you intend it to have? Did you conceive of it in sections? Two big halves? A series of numbered paragraphs? Any information about your first intentions as you may remember them can help jolt your memory, and remembering what you thought you were doing structurally is always crucial in revising. I can't tell you what the writers of the first three examples above had in mind, but the author of the fourth began with a set of premises about revision that became unworkable and needed to be rethought.[7]

Figure out what a book's subject is going to be. If you can think of a book project as a big block, hit it with a metaphysical hammer. Break it into pieces, something like five to ten, and give them names. When I write, I look for a kind of balance, a physical symmetry in the nonphysicality of the text, maybe because of the pleasure one finds in other forms of design and hopes to recreate on the page. I want the pieces of my writing to be roughly of equivalent size, and that in turn means that the pieces have to conceptualize aspects of the subject that are roughly equivalent in scope. It's a way of building from the outside in.

However you might have been thinking about structure when you began your draft, use revising as an opportunity

---

7. The running joke about revising a book on revising has been this writer's constant companion.

to rethink those assumptions. If they still work for you, then your task is determining whether you've used that structure in the best way possible. If those assumptions aren't working now—it's a different chapter or essay or article than you first thought it would be—look again at the structure of the draft.

Ask yourself these and any other questions that occur to you. You'll know better than anyone what dilemmas you face, what writerly evasions (most writers excel at writerly evasions) keep you from seeing straight ahead.

Here are two common evasions that may not look like evasions:

I've written this great paper. I'm going to use it.
I've just given this great talk. I'm going to use it.

The problem is a question of fit and audience, which is also a question of appropriate architecture.

The choices you made for your talk may have been exactly right for a talk, and the seminar paper that was roundly praised was a terrific seminar paper. That's great. But putting those successful performances to work in a larger project with different ambitions will change the calculus of their reception. What was applauded in front of a lecture hall won't feel the same on the page. If you're going to give your ideas the breathing room they require, you'll need to unlock those ideas from the structure of the talk or seminar paper, which now becomes not a set of bricks to be reassembled in a different location but part of your archive of ideas.

Thinking about how you will structure your writing is an opportunity to look at your working method and assumptions about shape:

What degree of structural transparency works for you?
Is the thing you're writing best presented with clinical speci-
   ficity?
Does it need numbered entries in short paragraphs?
Sections and subsections, with sequences clearly indicated?
Does your project require extended stretches of analysis?
How would you describe the structure—as separate from the
   content—of what you're writing?

Some forms of delivery emphasize the discreteness of elements. We've already looked at map and inventory as organizing principles. For some writers, these architectural markers are held quietly in reserve; for others, they need to be deliberately and visibly present in the text.

A lot of technical writing requires highly deliberate structuring of sections (e.g., systematic numbering: 1.1, 1.1a, 1.1b, 1.2; 2.1, 2.2, 2.3, etc.). Formal conventions dictate a tone and style intended to communicate analytic objectivity. Dry? Yes, often. If you want to repair a car or perform surgery or examine economic indicators, you're probably looking for facts, instructions, data. Nontechnical, or at least less technical, writing has other options.

One of the easiest, and most familiar, ways to develop the architecture of writing is the analytic skeleton. Topic, subtopics, sub-subtopics. Let's imagine a part of a book draft that the writer can organize in these terms, which are then displayed in the table of contents:

7   Why we fear rats
   7.1   Mythic conceptions
      7.1a   Folkloric associations
      7.1b   Comparison of European and non-
             European contexts

In this structure, the table of contents has functionally outlined the project for the reader. We're back to one of the points we looked at in the last chapter; here's a map (as opposed to an inventory) and the benefits of naming the component elements.

Note that the rule of thumb obligates you to have at least two subunits in any subordinate category. You can't have 7, 7.1, then 8. If you're tempted to produce one lonely subcategory, think again. It's a sure sign that you haven't figured out what goes where. A single subhead within a chapter looks less like subordinating than it suggests you haven't decided where your focus lies.

That requirement to have at least two subcategories isn't simply an arbitrary rule established by a cabal of prescriptivists. It's a way to achieve rhythm and balance in your writing. It's also a way of sparing you from awkwardly sticking on one additional observation in the guise of a subcategory.

You'll have noticed that the fragment in this example is organized both with a technical frame (1.1, etc.) and by means of concepts to be developed in narrative language. The skeleton is just that—a frame. The writer whose métier is narrative can go through this conceptual work and then pull the skeleton away, like a magician's disappearing act. If the writer has done it well, the text will have what will feel like natural rhythms, natural shifts. They will feel natural because they have been carefully planned for. Metaphor alert: organizing writing has a lot in common with organizing a garden. Formal patterns are grand; natural arrangements (which can take just as much work, though of a different kind) are grand, too.

Show your reader what you're up to. Try to act natural while you're doing it.

MAKING STRUCTURES VISIBLE

Architecture students spend years in the studio analyzing structures through the schematic lenses called *plan, elevation,* and *section.* In architecture lingo, a *plan* is a graphic representation that provides something like a perfect bird's-eye view of a structure. An *elevation* is a head-on view, something like looking perfectly at the front of a building. Architectural drawings can also be *sections,* cuts that slice through structures, the way an MRI scan slices through solid material to show an otherwise unavailable view.

Can we think about plan, elevation, and section as ways of conceptualizing the shape of writing? Maybe, though when writers talk about plans they usually have something else in mind. A scholarly writer's *plan* is a proposal, in greater or less detail, for something yet to be written. It has its own sense of architecture: a general announcement, a table of contents, an opening salvo meant to isolate a problem of sufficient interest to sustain the reader (and to convince the reader that it sustains the writer), and a series of chapters.[8] For the writer, a *section* usually means a smaller chunk of prose somewhere within a longer chunk of prose. Writing in *sections* that we call chapters—chapters that might, in turn, have further section subdivisions within them—is part of academic culture. Almost everyone who writes a schol-

---

8. Or sometimes a writer's *plan* is merely an intention: "I plan to use the summer to read deeply in my field." That's not the kind of plan we're focusing on here, though it sounds like a good use of your time.

arly book divides it up into its constituent elements and announces them on the contents page. As writers, we want—and need—those sections both to present our plan rapidly to potential readers, and to convince ourselves that we've organized things properly. We sometimes forget that last piece of the puzzle.

Take the architectural metaphors and put them to use. Reflect on the plan of your piece. Imagine a bird's-eye view. How to do that? This might be especially useful in long, i.e., book-length, projects. Can you write out an overview of your project that's at least something like the architect's understanding of a plan? Does your table of contents give you a responsible sense of what your book is going to do? Can you look at that table of contents as if it were literally a frontispiece—the front-facing surface of your structure—and get an understanding of what will be inside? What about the architectural section, that line of vision that moves through a project? Can you draw lines of ideas that move through your text? Do those lines help anchor together the pages of your work?

Writing can be like architecture, at least in some important ways, but we're working with words, and words are a difficult medium. If this were a more regular book about writing, you might expect here a series of pages on how long paragraphs should be, and whether or not a self-imposed limit on semi-colons is likely to sharpen your writing. (Quick answers: Shorter than they are in the draft you're working on. And yes.)

Or you might want a directive on how many chapters go into a book, how many pages can comfortably be nestled under a subsection head, how many subsection heads you need in a chapter. (Quick answers: As many as you need so that the reader will stay with you. At least three. At least two.)

Or how long a paper, or an article, or a book should be. (Honestly, those aren't questions for which anyone can give you a definitive answer. You'll almost always be working with guidelines. The academic world is big on guidelines, if not always strong on how to use them. Besides, the text you're writing is driven by *your* ideas, so you have to decide this one for yourself.)

But this isn't that book. Instead, let's think outside the manuscript box. Leonardo da Vinci—artist, designer, architect, inventor, draftsman, scientist, poster boy for Renaissance genius—understood the human body in itself and as a model of form. In one famous drawing, which you know even if you couldn't name it, Leonardo depicts a male figure inscribed in a circle: two superimposed frontal poses, four legs, four extended arms, as if the idealized proportion were some familiar yet unidentified deity. Leonardo used the image to demonstrate human proportions as corresponding to principles stated by Vitruvius, the first-century BC Roman writer on architecture.

The figure commonly referred to as "Vitruvian Man" man has seeped into popular culture as an iconic image of proportion and as a meme. But Leonardo's figure has always seemed to me to also be about centering the human subject and indicating the directions a life can and will go.

Thinking about Leonardo's figure, it struck me that there was a lesson here about writing, too. What goes into revising a piece of writing is also about the directions a draft can, and has to, go in pursuit of its ideas and its reader.

The page on which you write is a two-dimensional space, but nothing else about writing is. Let's borrow the idea from Leonardo and try to imagine a writer's draft in something like spatial terms. The metaphor doesn't work exactly, but stay with me.

5.1 Four revising directions.

Think of revising as looking both down and up, both across a span and outward into a beyond. This is revising in four directions and three dimensions (figure 5.1). *Revising up, revising down, revising across, revision out.* Let's get Vitruvian for a moment and see if we can find an unconventional way of imagining the rewriting process.

Revising is *revising up*, adding text. Why? Maybe because a reader of your manuscript, or you yourself, scribbles a note in the margin suggesting that maybe you want another category or another example, or maybe a better transition. Despite all the words on your pages, something is missing. You need more, maybe more and different. Revising up means filling the text out in some way. Another section, another paragraph, two more explanatory sentences, the missing chapter, another case study. Revising up is filling holes, adding a floor, constructing an extension.

When you read something and tell yourself that the argument and evidence are thin, you're sensing that the text needs more. So you add more. You'll do that to create greater continuity and persuasiveness, better connections and movement and flow. You'll be putting more meat on the bones, more wordy flesh on the skeleton of your idea, lending the reader a helping hand across a chasm you didn't know you'd left there. Revising up adds material, but not just any material. Not word count, but words that count, words that fill gaps in thought and make what you have to say easier to understand.

If you must add, remember to add cautiously. Productive expansion is almost never achieved simply by adding an example. Sometimes what's needed isn't Case Study #6 but a better, more slowly built set-up. If all else fails, rephrase and repeat, though not so obviously that you insult the reader. You know a lot. But knowing when to deliver less than you know and doing it succinctly is a precious writerly art. The reader is not your research file and doesn't want to be. Don't be a firehose.

Revising down has similar goals: refining style while achieving greater clarity and persuasiveness, but in this case by boiling away everything that doesn't contribute to the work that needs to get done. The most famous book on writing well may be Strunk and White's *The Elements of Style*, which William Strunk Jr. first devised a century ago.[9] You'll already know Professor Strunk's "no useless words" mantra. But the question is always, which words are they?

Successful writing doesn't compress everything, but the successful writer has a sense of where to move quickly and where not so quickly, where to summarize and where to luxuriate in detail. There are famous writers who are all laconic compression, others whose prose practically has tendrils winding around a sun-bleached subject. Compression is an element of pacing. It's a skill, to be used sparingly, but it's critical to establish the rhythm of one's writing and the effective display of an argument or idea.

If you're revising a long piece, revising down begins with identifying what your inner voice tells you is the extraneous example, the analysis that repeats, the point that is underlined three times when twice is quite enough.

Academic writers can be especially nervous about word count. Is it long enough? is it too long? Of course, there are

9. *The Elements of Style*, 4th ed. (London: Pearson, 2019).

situations in which limits are understood (the journal accepts submissions between eight thousand and ten thousand words in length) or contractually agreed (the publisher wants a 65,000-word manuscript, and while there might be some wiggle room, it's unlikely that 25,000 or 125,000 words will satisfy). Word counts are helpful—I use them myself—but I try hard never to let "hitting the quota" persuade me that I've written something well. Try to concentrate on what you have to say and less on the number of words you take to say it. Once you've said it, though, see how many words it took.

Every guide to writing has something to say about clarity and effectiveness, and how to get to those admirable qualities. The suggestion is often that shorter is going to be better, more effective writing. Writing can, in fact, work that way, but scholarly writing is often charged with a responsibility for detail and thoroughness that works against the shorter-is-better mantra. *There's no law that says revising a text is essentially cutting that text back.* Sometimes you need more.

Writing rule: You can't know what's missing until you know what you're looking for to begin with.

Yes, revising involves cutting, adding, and changing your words, but attention to extraction and patching in new sentences and paragraphs can be a distraction from the process we've been looking at: learning what you already have—and being sure that what you have is what you want. Only then look at the gaps and redundancies. When you find them, make them go away. Look at a clean page. Read it out loud. If you've done your chimney sweeping well, you'll like what you hear.

Writing rule: Aim to shape positively, even when you're removing words.

Before shortening an overlong paragraph or chapter,

mark up what's of value. A concept, a clause, a string of paragraphs in the middle of a fifty-page stretch of prose. Mark up with an electronic highlighting function or with pencil on paper, but identify the best bits visually. Who knows when you'll get back to the pages you're working on? Even if you put the draft aside for one day or several, you'll be glad to return to a document with mark-ups.

Revising up extends and relaxes a text by adding what's missing. Revising down applies verbal economy to consolidate your ideas and increase their effectiveness. It's not a matter of choosing between these modes. When you revise, you'll be doing both at once, scraping away redundancy, replacing weak formulations with stronger ones, and finding better words, sharper explanations, more precise ways to make a point.

Writing rule: Read your shortened version against the longer, original version. The shortened version needs to feel just as strong but more effective.

Revising across is a way to think about internal coherence. A different outside reader sends you this note. "I think I see what you want to say here, but does this bit on page 18 follow the argument on 17 or is it really closer to what you say on page 36? Also, is the series of paragraphs on page 58 the opposite of what you say on page 20?"

Your reader has helped you discover that you haven't arranged everything in the right order yet. Sometimes that's what's meant when a journal responds with the phrase "revise and resubmit." It's the almost-amber light of academic journalese: we don't hate it and we want to love it; now please strengthen it and knock on our door again. Or maybe your draft has come back with less thoroughly laid-out responses. A red pen merely notes a reaction: "Huh?" "I've no idea what this means." Brusque, yes, but the point is made: there are questions about coherence, about the way in which the pieces are attached to one another, about the way ideas seem to be flung at the reader.

Revising across is rethinking the big embrace that any piece of writing pledges to sustain: "I the author promise to make these sentences and paragraphs into a coherent picture of an idea." Revising across is a bit like revising up. Both directional gestures are about smoothing out the steps from one idea to the next. Revising up fills in the gaps, while revising across makes sure the pieces within your writing add up, connect to the pieces that precede and follow them, and have only one possible order.

Good writing is coherent writing. But coherence is a tricky concept. The larger the thing you're writing, the greater the risk that coherence can slip between your fingers, that the components won't feel connected, that they'll seem juxtaposed rather than developed each from the component that precedes it.

Revising out shifts the camera away from you and your words and toward your readers. This directional signal is a reminder that all the work you've put into your revision is on behalf of the unseen, unknowable reader in your head. You're not just writing. You're making something.

Especially in the case of book-length projects, it can be hard to remember that, while you're writing a manuscript, you're also building a little world made up of ideas, perceptions, arguments, evidence, data. The larger your writing project, the greater the danger that, at least from the reader's perspective, pieces of the whole may not hold together. Revise your text, buckling its sections to one another, and do it in order to revise outward, too. Build a text that acknowledges and enfolds its reader.

BUILDING TECHNIQUES

Different writers have different writing habits and styles, and they will have different habits and styles of revising, too. Some work in pieces, taking multiple printouts and spreading them across a table. Some save everything to well-organized electronic files, nimbly toggling between multiple screens to compare multiple versions. Some revisers work with many versions and choose the best parts from each. Some work with one version and then its replacement. Some writers add sections. Others scour and re-scour a passage, adding words one at a time, now here, now there, until not a single sentence remains exactly as it was first written. I'm sympathetic to the scourer, since I'm one of them.

Structures count. But as with everything else about writing, there's a catch. As writers, we tell ourselves a lot of things about what we're writing and why we're writing it. Most writers think that their chapters are already elements that are at once both independent and part of the big picture. ("Isn't my structure obvious? It's got chapters!") But one of the most common faults in structuring a book is believing that because a text is in chapters it already has a viable architecture.

Division into chapters can be a tautological error. The definition of a chapter isn't eight thousand sequential words of a larger text (the text is a loaf of bread, and a chapter is a slice). Nor is it eight thousand sequential words exhaustively examining something (one slice of bread, crumb by crumb).

Parts need to be ordered and to have a purpose; otherwise, what the writer takes to be a wall is a pile of bricks, discrete and unordered. We've all read books that are a series of semi-independent essays, which is fine if that's what the writer has promised and the publisher was happily expecting, but that kind of structure has to be clearly intended from the beginning, not something the reader backs into, much less a structure that the writer believes is unified, coherent, and connected—what in music might be called a *durchkomponiertes Werk*—a through-composed work, something not broken into pieces but continuously scrolling onward to its finale. A book of essays doesn't try to do that. A book with chapters does.

Some writers want to marry chapters. Is anyone ever really persuaded by a table of contents that divvies up a small number of chapters into pairs that are then labeled "Parts" or "Sections"? Those labels are just window-dressing. Ditto "interludes" and other interstitial fragments. Ask yourself: "What would such a structure accomplish that I could do by means of a more consistent flow of ideas?" If you're inclined to marry chapters, take a moment to see if what you're really responding to is the need to do more work on revising across.

Everything true about the big picture of writing is true of the small picture, too. All that we've considered so far about purpose, problem, and structure insofar as it applies to a book-length manuscript is also relevant to the individual chapter. The mapping exercises we looked at earlier in this book, especially the Writing Bullseye subject-problem-question exercise, are applicable to the largest units of a full-length work.

So an architectural review of a draft might yield both a big picture and specific, local insights.

This section does not follow from that.
This paragraph needs to be moved from page 4 to page 2.
Was this paragraph an error—maybe a relic of an earlier draft?
*The fourth paragraph on page 9 repeats a point better made in
    the second paragraph on page 5.*
Does that sentence belong here?

Chapter 6 needs to follow chapter 3, and a topic completely absent in the first draft needs to be written and located as a new chapter 4.

It's all about shape and consequence.

Good writing takes risks and shows the way. Keep an eye out for the moments where your reader needs you to explain. Writers are diggers, builders, artists, mapmakers. The best scholarly writing, though, might just be more cartographic than archaeological, more about showing new routes and the shape of the coast than digging things up and dusting them off. Aim to strike the balance that's right for what you're writing and of most use to your reader.

If this sounds like a new way of thinking about writing, that might be a good thing. Gertrude Stein, modernist poet and cryptic forger of bon mots, once asked, "If it can be done, why do it?" Stein wasn't telling us to be lazy. Just the opposite. She wanted to urge the embrace of the impossible.

Stein is tonic, but you can't live on a diet of tonic. On the other hand, you don't have to go full Aristotle to concede that something written has a beginning, a middle, and an end.

Some writers begin at the beginning and write out a draft straight through. Other writers start almost anywhere in a project, moving backward and forward. We all write sometimes in the first mode and sometimes in the second. In writing or revising, a system can help. Here's a simple one that I find especially helpful: the Writing W (figure 5.2).

One of the most recognizable shapes in the night sky is the constellation Cassiopeia, or the Wain.

"Wain" is an older word for wagon, the sort of simple cart in which a farmer might have moved hay back when John Constable was painting the English countryside. The

5.2 Cassiopeia; or, The Wain.

Writing **W** is a sort of wagon for your ideas, a schematic structure that sequences elements of writing in a slightly counterintuitive way. The diagram represents the order in which you might write a draft.

What's the logic here? You want to make an immediate connection between your first intuition, that original idea that you hope will prove to be a generational insight, and your conclusion, which you expect to make convincingly available to your reader. *Making your conclusion convincingly available to your reader.* That's a state of play that's related to persuasive argument, but it's more than that. It's making the persuasive argument meaningful to the audience you want to reach.

In the Writing **W** model, you track your idea by following the **W**'s strokes (figure 5.3).[10] You do something at each of the letter's five points.

Here's the strategy:

Star 1 (upper left). Write this first. Lay out your opening move, including your argument or significant position.
Star 2 (lower left). The end of the first stroke is the end of your essay. Write your conclusion now. Yes, now.
Star 3 (center). Now, in the fat middle of the **W**, you put

10. The **W** model grew out of my experience teaching first-year students at Cooper Union. I particularly want to thank engineering student Jason He for his contribution to that class discussion.

everything you need to support your argument and
move you toward your conclusion (which you've already
written in this draft, so you have some idea of what
you're aiming at). The two middle strokes in the **W** stand
for the midpoint in all that evidence-gathering and arranging, but don't fuss too much about the symbolism.

Star 4 (lower right). Back to your conclusion. Rewrite it so
that it makes sense based on what's happened in the big
developmental stage.

Star 5 (upper right). Return to the beginning and carefully
review every word in your opening paragraph. Adjust it
the way you adjust seasonings before serving a dish to
company.

This is about as far from the five-paragraph essay as you can
get. Instead of doing that five-paragraph thing—emphasizing
the Three Examples that prove what you've said and will say
again—it emphasizes the pairing of beginning and ending *as*
beginning. Superficial, you say? Yes, and proud of it; nothing
in the **W** model works against the importance of evidence. It
just obliges you to figure out what you're trying to do. Here's
that order again:

1 Opening
2 Conclusion
3 The entirety of the body text
4 Conclusion, again
5 Opening, again

By the time you've finished, you'll know where you wanted to start.

The point here is that the architecture of an essay or chapter, or any reasonably containable unit of prose with ideas in it, is a process as much as it is a form. Make that work for you. You'll probably discover that some aspects of structure become less or more important, depending on the kind of writing you're working on. I'll end this chapter by pointing out some features of writing's architecture that challenge us all.

TIME'S UP

Julian Barnes used the phrase "the sense of an ending" as the title of a 2011 novel which, being a novel, has a lot to do with memory. The critic Frank Kermode used the same phrase as the title of a set of lectures on the apocalyptic in the literary imagination. We might use the phrase yet again to ask ourselves, "When should a piece of writing end? And how?" Or, to look at it from a different angle, "Did that ending make any sense?"

As you revise an ending, take a moment to review your writing with these features in mind:

Deferral. Yes, delay can be a structural pleasure for the reader, and for the writer, too. Deferral means extending a discussion or an analysis, or any part of your writing that constitutes the head and body (but not the tail) long enough that when you get to the point you want to deliver, there is anticipation, and then, finally, delivery. This isn't the same as having a punchline. Like compression and expansion (revising down, revising up), deferral is about pacing, achieving the feeling that the writing knows where it wants to go and how fast the writer needs to go to get it there. Writing isn't just about beginnings. It's about arrival, too.

The off-ramp. One of revision's objectives is to find the best way out of a piece of writing. That can feel like looking for an exit sign in a dark space. Even practiced, professional writers can find the last sentences of a piece of writing the most difficult to compose. If you're writing a five-hundred-word op-ed piece for the local newspaper, the rightness of your last sentence may depend more on delivering a memorable punch than on recalibrating the argument you've quickly tried to build up. In a scholarly essay or a book-length manuscript, knowing where to stop and what to say when you get there is trickier. It's the last gesture, the last backward glance at the reader and the subject before the writer disappears. Whatever else those final sentences and paragraphs do, the writer wants to be sure that they leave the reader with ideas and tools for thinking. Hasn't that been the objective of your writing project?

Conclusions. These connect finding the off-ramp of writing back to the fundamental concept of usability and the take-away that we've been looking at throughout this book. Conclusions are about work done and work *to be done.* The end of a project can be a moment for summation, a grand gathering up of the writer's findings, hopes, fears, and dreams. But a conclusion doesn't have to be any of those things. A complex piece of writing may be able to deliver its conclusions along the way, as implications and inferences and warnings. That might make it possible for the last chunk of a text to be placid and redundant. Or truly speculative, even counterintuitive.

There are so many ways to end a piece of writing that it would be hard to produce any sort of meaningful catalogue.

But we can say that endings are affected by genre and intention and tone, by writerly skill, and by dumb luck.

The secret of conclusions—and like all secrets of writing they're there for anyone to see—is that the ending of a work has multiple obligations. However the writer chooses to fulfill them, what's most important is their order of priority: conclusions are there first for *the writer's ideas*, then for the *reader*, and last of all for the *writer*. Whatever happens in the conclusion of a piece of writing, then, must be primarily motivated by the desire to serve the piece's ideas. You, and even your reader, have to wait.

From this perspective, writing is like having a child or other dependent, or living with what we used to call a pet and might now call one's companion animal. When you make the commitment to enlarge your family unit, you gain by giving up. You enrich your life by attending to another living thing, and at least sometimes putting that other's priorities ahead of your own.

When you're really *really* writing, you disappear into your material. And not just into your material, but into the life of your ideas, the struggles that rage around the problem you have happily invented. You write, of course, for your reader, and—let it not go without saying—at some level all writers write for themselves. But the foundational engagement of writing, what we might call the Primary Dialogue, is between the writer and the writer's ideas. Everything else is secondary, because if the Primary Dialogue is weak, or dull, or doesn't exist—if either your idea or you yourself is a bad conversationalist—then there's nothing else to work for, or with. So the ending of a piece of writing should somehow acknowledge the piece's central idea, as well as the purpose of putting it out into the world.

After that, the conclusion is there for the reader. If the writer has got the ideas sorted, and the reader has been attentively cared for from the first paragraph to the last, the conclusion will speak to the reader easily. Nothing further will be required.

And what about the writer? What's in it for her or him? Writing is finally, inevitably, *about* the writer but not *for* the writer. The writing comes out of the writer; its ideas are the writer's gift to the world.

So at some level, everything you write is a piece of an extended autobiography, but that doesn't mean it's your present to yourself about yourself. It's autobiography because it's taken up so much of your life and because the very fact of your interest in a subject fleshes out some feature of your intellectual—and maybe even emotional—make-up. What you write is about something that is not you, and just a little bit about you, too.

The Psalmist tells us that for everything there is a season. A time to plant and a time to reap, and so forth; five centuries of Bible translation have let the beauty of Hebrew's balanced line shine out in memorable English. Verily, there's a time to revise and a time to stop revising. Knowing when to stop is going to be a test of the writer's patience and instinct and energy. These work together. In revising, what we call instinct is a combination of things: knowing whether you have more to say or are out of ideas; knowing whether you have time left to continue reorganizing or amplifying or cutting; and knowing whether you have the stomach for it.

In the 1950s, George Plimpton interviewed Ernest Hemingway. This exchange was part of their discussion:

Hemingway: I rewrote the ending to *A Farewell to Arms*, the last page of it, thirty-nine times before I was satisfied.

Plimpton: Was there some technical problem there? What was it that had stumped you?

Hemingway: Getting the words right.

Successful revision *can* mean bringing what you're writing to a state that feels, at least now, like the best thing you've ever done. But successful revision *doesn't have to feel like that.*

It's not just that we're not all Hemingways (never a goal of mine, by the way). At some point, you can't revise any further, and you shouldn't. It may not be perfect, just very much better than when you began. Sometimes a writer works and works and works to get something exactly the way it has to be.

Experienced writers understand that there are limits that bound all writers, whatever their talents and ambitions, whatever their fields and genres. Toni Morrison holds a special place for her experience at Random House, where the author of *The Bluest Eye* held down a day job in publishing and wrote in whatever time was left over. Morrison is the rare example of a great writer who got to see the writing process from all its angles.

Morrison once acknowledged that she'd revised something she'd been working on "six times, seven times, thirteen times" (so you can hardly complain about a fourth run-through of your own text). It's a good reminder that revision sometimes means going back again and again and again. But she also offered advice we can all take to heart: Revise, but don't fret. "There's a line," Morrison says, "between revision and fretting, just working it to death. It is better to know when you are fretting it; when you are fretting it because it is not working, it needs to be scrapped."[11]

11. "The Art of Fiction No. 134," *Paris Review*, no. 128 (Fall 1993).

"Fretting when it's not working." Writing has to work, and to *do* work. If you can't make it work, either for yourself or for your reader, you need another gear or piston instead of the one you've been trying to fix.

I don't like to scrap work. I'll do whatever I can to salvage or repurpose pages that I recognize aren't working where I'd put them. Sometimes the solution is to make more, smaller sections so that I have the opportunity for more conclusions or cadences, more, smaller finales, more off-ramps. When a scrapped sentence turns out to be the solution to an unfinished section, that's a kind of writerly magic. Writing doesn't end once; it ends over and over again, which means the writer has opportunities over and over again to land an idea. How we end a chapter or a long section of writing can be among our most influential writerly moments. Metaphor from gymnastics: the routine can dazzle with its high-flying demonstrations of courage and skill, but much depends on nailing the dismount.

Morrison's wise caution not to overdo it is as sensible as it is unscientific. There's no meter that will tell you when to stop revising. You'll have to know it for yourself. To stick the dismount, you have first to commit yourself to there being a dismount.

MAKE USEFUL SHAPES

In the *Thomas the Tank Engine* children's books, Thomas and his locomotive pals are called the Really Useful Engines. (With a nod to Thomas, the composer Sir Andrew Lloyd-Webber named his production company the Really Useful Group.) Good architecture in writing is useful. Really useful.

Good, useful architecture happens when the shape of the

writing supports the writing's ideas. That's partly a matter of mechanics and building materials. Writing structures build confidence. You want a reader to feel that the hands putting the text together are skilled hands. That the shape of ideas will run clearly. That beginnings will begin and endings will end, and that the pieces will connect. You want a structure that will keep your prose and your readers safe.

The shape of a piece of writing will always be perceived as of secondary importance to the ideas within it. That makes architecture a kind of secret weapon. When you set up headings, when you take deliberate control of the length of paragraphs, when you make your openings and closings as effective as you can, you're shaping your text and the reader's response to your text.

Structure in writing isn't a frozen thing, any more than moving through a wonderful piece of architecture means being glued to one spot, eyes straight ahead. We may not always think of it that way, but human movement through a built environment is itself a structural component of a building's design.

Structures speak to many needs, including the need for movement. Let's hold on to that comparison of the structure of the built environment to the structure made of language and reflect on those two structures, not as static, but as dynamic. The dynamic experience of reading something has to be built into a writer's structure of words, sentences, paragraphs, and chapters. Structure, then, is both a solid thing and a fluid thing, as space is both a place and a movable placement within it.

At the top of this chapter, I said that good architects are responsive to the needs of the site (the location, the relation to earth and sky as well as other structures) and to the needs of the community that will use the structure. A good architect wouldn't concentrate on a structure to the exclusion of the people who are meant to use and move through it.

Communities, inhabitants, readers. Build the right house: as you architect your own writing, focus on who you're inviting to use it. Which is why the most important of the three A's, to which we now turn, is audience.

6

Remember the audience

Writing isn't a job for cynics. If you believe that "nobody reads anymore," why would you spend time writing? Why *revise* for nobody?

In fact, reading isn't what it used to be, but on balance that might be a very good thing. We have access to so much more, and so much more easily. I can work on digitized files from international collections, download scholarly articles through JSTOR, leverage my college library to access necessary reference works, read free downloads made available by generous publishers and authors, and buy Kindle editions of most everything. More to the point: I can do this while sitting at a little table at home, watching pigeons and occasional other birds I fail to identify but am happy to see stopping by.

The field of book history explores the future of the book and the future of reading, which means it's a field about readers. The printed book is more than merely a technology; it's *also* merely a technology. The book or the journal or the newspaper is a technological conveyance, and in the digital era we now have more conveyances. Digital conveyances are faster, more fluid, in some ways more portable. In other ways, not. A paperback book is hard to beat.[1]

Yes, we read differently. Facts that were once hard to find, if they could be found at all, are now online and available in a few seconds of searching. We teach differently now. We write differently, too. A reader's attention is a more fragile thing, not because today's readers didn't read the books you read (or experience the youth you experienced), but because we now swim in information, and writing is more like a school of fish than an island destination. Porous, quick-changing, open to infinite opportunity: the reader who turns to what you're writing is making a specific, self-limiting choice. Writing for a reader now isn't the same as writing for a reader in the 1950s or the 1850s. More than ever, reading is a game for partners.

What remains constant, though, is the human need to communicate through language and writing. Not just communicate *from* but communicate *to*. When I teach workshops on scholarly writing, I often say that what I'm preaching is "baby phenomenology" (I'm not sure that's what it is, but it's what I call it). The principle goes like this: *It's not what I say that counts. It's what you hear.*

People often chuckle, and I hope they're laughing because it rings true. But there's a truth in it that goes to the heart of revising writing. It's not the research and the knowledge, the judicious sifting, the care with which you've organized your findings that counts. It's what your reader takes away. Maybe not quickly, maybe not in a single reading. Maybe only through repeated engagements with your carefully made

1. Among the many books exploring what a book might be, see Leah Price, *What We Talk about When We Talk about Books* (New York: Basic, 2019), and Amaranth Borsuk, *The Book* (Cambridge, MA: MIT Press, 2018).

written object. But as you'll well know by now, the point of revising writing is to get your reader to engage. No engagement, no reader, and your work sits there. Keats's chilling phrase "cinders, ashes, dust" describes the fate of starving lovers.[2] The unread book is a sad thing, too, and just as dusty.

Everything we've looked at so far—getting to grips with what you're trying to communicate, figuring out a structure that supports and displays what you're saying—turns on the importance of the reader. Although you may never meet any of them, your readers are your audience. You write for them. You definitely revise for them. You just can't see them.

That invisibility means you've got to prepare as best you can. For writers building a project out of scholarly research, it's asking a lot for them to set the reader ahead of, say, a juicy (at least to the writer) discovery or a powerful (at least to the writer) theory. A challenge, yes. But nothing outweighs the reader.

To be clear, this isn't a swipe at discovery or theory, which are at the heart of scholarly writing. It's not a criticism of meticulous, detailed specialist research, either. It's a plea, and one that this book has made repeatedly, for tempering the analytic and archaeological with a commitment to narrative, whatever you're writing.

A narrative is a kind of thread, but not every thread is a narrative. When people talk about writing, they talk a lot about threads running through a text and connecting its ideas. Has the word *thread* ever been more visible than it is now, in the age of social media, not even discounting the heyday of weaving mills? We're invited to link email chains or to see the spidery filament of responses to a particularly arch

2. *Lamia* (1820), Part 2, l. 2.

tweet, so that we've normalized "thread" as a term for and of connection. The thread is the name for the mechanical linkages connecting post to post.

Journalists, who know the importance of developing a story out of reportage and reportage out of facts and observations, might be tempted to *storify* the events being covered. Social media fans have been tempted to arrange tweets and other micro-communications into a "story," or at least into some sort of sequence from which a narrative line might be inferred.[3]

A thread can be the slimmest of connections and, like Hansel and Gretel's bread crumb trail into and out of the forest, that might be enough (or would have been, had birds not eaten the crumbs). Story or narrative does more. Things happen. Actors do things. Bread crumbs are a thread. Two kids lost in a forest is the set-up for a narrative. In a narrative, actions have consequences.

Narrative, storytelling, the drama inherent in one's subject: readers read to know what happens next, what idea follows from the previous one, how a theory sends out its tendrils to establish itself in the world. To write well, listen to the elements in your text, not just to the words but also to the actors, the concepts, the noises in your argument.

Why this insistence upon listening? Because whatever you have to say in print or online, whatever effort a publisher takes to put what you've said so well into an accessible format, nothing happens until there's a reader.

"Remember the audience" isn't like "Remember your password." Remembering your audience requires *forward*

---

3. *Storify* was also the name of a web-based organizer that, from 2011 to 2018, aimed to help users create "stories" out of social media postings.

memory. You remember that they're out there when you do whatever you can to prepare for their arrival. Remembering the audience is like getting ready for company. Eager, curious, judgmental company.

Readers change what publishers publish and writers write. Ever jot a note in the margins of a book? Sometimes we do that to correct a typo. Sometimes to remind ourselves that a particular passage is one we want to come back to. Sometimes we do more: we *write back* to the author, arguing a different perspective or, sometimes, proposing our own, better wording. Ever mark up a digital copy with your own counterarguments? That's a sign of a reader thinking about what the writer has put on the page, and isn't that just what a writer wants? Looked at this way, what the writer publishes is somewhere between declaration and suggestion, maybe less like a formal document and more like a performer's script.

The thing you're writing, the text you've worked so hard to nail down safely, is suddenly something less permanent, something open to interpretation. Texts move, shift, become a thing the reader makes, based on the thing the writer makes.

If that's true, then everything you do as a writer is keyed to making it possible for the reader to do something with what you've written. And if you take that seriously, the result can make a big difference not only in how you write but in what you write. The choice of topic, the approach, the shape of the thing you make, the way you package your ideas and set out a path for the reader to follow. The way you revise, the way you refine shape and structure in order to make it easier for the eager reader to come in and stay a while.

Writing for an audience doesn't mean imagining thousands of people somewhere. That's an abstract and, frankly, pretty useless concept. Instead, imagine writing for one real, not-at-all abstract, interested reader, and then for another real reader, and another, and another.

Those readers aren't clones, either. They're unique. If you're a writer, you're trying to reach each of those unique readers, real and unknown. So how do you get to the audience, whoever it may be?

If you've been clarifying your argument, you've done it so that you can finally know, as sharply as possible, the point you want to make. And so your reader will know the point you want to make.

Again and again, you've restructured your prose and rethought its architecture. You've been doing this to make your argument clearer, and so your reader will feel invited in, made comfortable, and supported, even when being challenged. Should you challenge your reader? Of course. But at some level you've got to give readers what they want.

WHAT READERS WANT

What *do* readers want, exactly? Pleasure? Excitement? Provocation? A good fight? The answer? Here are some things readers look for.

1. Something to chew on. Crudely put, a reader wants an idea. All by itself, an idea probably isn't a book, or even an essay, but an essay or book without an idea is going to be frustrating. The reader needs to feel that there's substance in your writing, and that the substance is worth spending time thinking about. Some perfectly respectable manuscripts do everything except explain what's at stake and why the reader should care. However you choose to do it, make clear to your readers what it's all worth, to you and to them.

2. Something to make the reader turn the page. There are a lot of ways to think about the reasons people read, but if you're writing something in prose, count on the reader wanting an interesting story, regardless of the subject. True, there are plenty of topics that don't seem immediately amenable to "story," but work to find a connection that will hold your reader's attention anyway.

Stories depend on sequence. Even stories told out of sequence are just following sequence 2.0. Write as if your reader will encounter each of your pages in the order in which you've placed them, but don't be surprised if your reader skims or jumps around. That doesn't mean that you're a bad writer or that your reader's lazy or inattentive.

Haven't you ever skimmed something to find out the conclusion? Fast-forwarded through a whodunit to find out who's the guilty party? Or simply jumped from a scholarly article's abstract to the final subhead, conveniently called "Conclusions"? The team of writers who assembled the data that went into those conclusions worked hard to provide the details, and in a sequence that would be logical and persuasive. That's a kind of story that even quantitative analysts can take seriously. Explaining a research method and protocol and then the outcome of the experiment creates a kind of narrative, if only we think of it that way. Telling a story, sustaining an argument, developing a character all depend on extension and duration, even in a work of academic analysis. You can't force your reader to read every page in order, but if you write as if that's the way a reader will read, you'll have made the best case for deserving a reader's attention.

3. Your attention. Speaking of which, a reader wants your attention. That may sound backward, but think of it this way: if you write, you're asking your readers for some of their time,

time they could easily spend on anything else. You're not just providing them with a text; you're inviting them *into* the text. Be a good host. Pay attention. Refill glasses. Pass the nibbles.

Good teachers, after all, don't just demand attention. They pay attention. Scholarly writers are teachers *all the time*, not only when they're online in a Zoom class session or at a blackboard in a physical meeting room.

It's never enough for academic writing simply to declare and provide ample supporting details, even if that feels like the foundational gesture of scholarship. There's a small irony here. What scholars are good at, really good at, is paying attention, seeing the detail that's slipped through the cracks, putting two and two together and discovering that four is just one possible solution (how is three plus one different?), going back over an old problem with new methods (digital analytics, cutting-edge technologies, social theories) to see what couldn't be seen before.

Anyone who works in the humanities will have internalized the value of "close reading." It wouldn't be much of a stretch to say that all scholarly research, in any field, is some form of close reading. "What do you do for a living?" someone asks a scholarly researcher. "I pay attention—professionally," comes the reply.

Good writing, and especially good scholarly writing, happens when the last bit of attention is paid and the reader is moved into the center of the project.

Paying attention to your reader can require several things. Getting the tone of the project right means figuring out what degree of casualness and formality you need in order to deliver the goods. Scholarly writing has an implicit contract with its readers: the writer has something to say that the readers don't know (otherwise why would they bother reading it?), but the writer is also depending on the readers' familiarity with enough of the history or context to make sense of, and use, what the writer has to say.

And that's where it can get tricky. You want to acknowledge that the reader knows what you are assuming the reader knows, but you want to do it without making a fool of yourself, or of your reader. Of course, you'll never intentionally write something that sounds disdainful and superior. Readers aren't stupid. They don't want to feel they're being condescended to. But it's OK to use ordinary, everyday language if you can do it in a way that feels natural to your subject and its disciplinary readership. Instinct sometimes skews toward the demotic; if ordinary languages feels right to you, be bold. In fact, the more you can say about your subject or question in ordinary language, the larger your readership is likely to be. The more specialized your language, the more specialized (read: small) your readership. Writers make choices. They have to.

As you read a draft out loud, listen especially to any moment where you hear the possibility of being misinterpreted. There's no guarantee that you'll prevent every potential misunderstanding, but if you set yourself the task, you'll have a much better chance of avoiding this pitfall.

4. The dots connected. In the last chapter, we looked at structure and how the structure isn't a consequence of argument but at least a codeterminant. Give your reader links from chapter to chapter and section to section.

Don't write seventy-five-page chapters, which will only suggest that the project's structure hasn't been well thought out. ("I have more to say" is not an argument for another twenty pages.) Think about how much time you expect your reader to spend with your chapter. A rule of thumb: a chapter is a sustained component, meant to be read at one sitting, of a larger, multicomponent project. It's fine to depend on your reader's *sitzfleisch*, a term we might translate as "stubborn gluteal endurance," but it's generous not to impose unreasonably on said fleisch.

5. Smoothness. When the dots are well connected, the reader can follow the writing without unnecessary distraction. Some writers on writing talk about "smoothness." The term was part of English usage for centuries before data analytics brought the concepts of smoothness and smoothing into widespread use. Smoothing functions allow us to get a better sense of a data set without the distraction of the irregularities we perceive as noise. Like data analysts, readers want access to arguments and ideas with only minimal distraction from noise.

But readers want a *living* voice on the page or on the screen. They want to hear language that moves smoothly, and one of the ways it moves smoothly is because it has just a bit more verbiage in it than might be absolutely required.

Here's a test. Take any paragraph you've written. Rewrite it with the fewest possible words. You'll have produced something like the writerly equivalent of freeze-dried food: the nutrients might remain, but the result doesn't exactly cry out to be tasted. Compare that freeze-dried paragraph to your original. What's in the original that you pulled away? Not redundant or otherwise unnecessary language, exactly, but enough to hydrate it. Those hydrating touches enliven prose, engage the reader, and create an ease of access we can think of as smoothness. They're only useless words if they're useless to you.

These features of responsible writing reflect a writer's view of the reader as smart, interested, and present. Would you have it any other way?

Readers, in other words, are people just like you but who are not you. They want to be engaged, respected, and treated with generosity. Listen to what you want from what you read. Try to make as much of that available to your readers as you can. Line up your best arguments, your best thinking, the examples you need. Cut the examples, thinking, arguments that you don't. What ties that all together? Something that gets called voice.

YOUR WRITING VOICE

Voice is an elusive concept in scholarly writing, but it can make or break a book's reception. What sort of voice are you writing in? Authoritative voice? (Save it for when you need it most, and remember not to yell. Loud isn't authoritative; it's just loud.) Collegial voice? (Don't be too informal or you'll undercut your authority.) Nonspecialist voice? (Yes, for nonspecialist readers, but sparingly for specialists.) Are you writing as an attack dog? (Sometimes that's what's necessary.) As the peacemaker in a fractious debate? (You're a genuinely good person, at least at this moment.) Is your voice personal, intimate, confessional? (Good, but what are you getting for all that self-exposure?)

Voice involves position, perspective, attitude, and the way you say what you have to say. It's the sound you choose to make, and that's the sum or consequence of all of those things. When you pay careful attention to all the possible style features at your fingertips—word choices, matters of tone and volume, sense of formality and informality, and so on—you're paying attention to voice.

Voice is critical, but why is it so elusive? When writers on writing say something about what makes a book work, the first thing they emphasize is often the writer's voice. My hunch is that they emphasize voice so much exactly because it's so difficult to identify.

And I don't blame them. There are lots of serious discussions about writing and voice, almost all of it focused on writers of fiction. Julie Wildhaber, dispensing online advice as Grammar Girl, offers a lively take: voice is "the distinct personality, style, or point of view of a piece of writing or any other creative work." She explains:

> Voice is important because your writing should have as much personality as you do. You've read things that seem to have been written by committee, and it's not a fun experience. A strong voice helps you make every word count, establish consistency across your website or body of work, and most importantly helps you grab your readers' attention and establish a relationship with them.[4]

Wildhaber's sensible encouragement may need a bit of parsing for academic writers. We're nervous about grabbing attention. We're very nervous about fun. But academic writers also know, better than many readers, what it's like to read work written by committee. Voice is the human feeling, the personality, the sense of presence that animates the words you write. One wants to say to writers, and especially to scholarly writers, "Write humanely."

So what would writing humanely sound like? A natural feel but not a cute or gimmicky or folksy feel, because for academic writers those writing moves can come off as insincere, even condescending. It isn't easy to be natural on

---

4. https://www.quickanddirtytips.com/education/grammar/under standing-voice-and-tone-in-writing.

the page, much less to be natural, scholarly, methodical, and persuasive. But that's the task.[5]

This hard-won naturalness is the art that conceals art. And difficult as it is, that's the necessary condition that allows for the widest possible readership to engage with what the writer has written.

Yet in the matter of voice, it often seems that academics are encouraged to be discouraged. *Not so loud. Somebody might hear you behind your prose.* Don't we all know that we're expected to sound official, professional, neutral? Well, maybe.

The idea of a writer's voice feels more natural, easier to achieve, when talking about books for a general audience than it does when we're talking about academic prose. Scholars have always had an anxious relationship to the idea of voice, as if something so important to trade books couldn't, or shouldn't, also be important to academic writers.

"Write like *that?*" you might find yourself thinking, as if there's an academic version of theater's fourth wall. But it's possible to be analytic and present on the page, possible to hold up the value of objectivity and be a person who is writing and holding up that value.

There are scholars whose writing skill and ambition have allowed them to move from research monograph to prize-winning nonfiction bestseller. There are scholars who have shifted their energies from scholarship qua scholarship, re-training in fiction or mixed genres that call into question the comfort of boundaries.

5. On the weird power of the cute, the gimmick, and other easily overlooked phenomena, see Sianne Ngai, *Our Aesthetic Categories: Zany, Cute, Interesting* (Cambridge, MA: Harvard University Press, 2015) and *Theory of the Gimmick: Aesthetic Judgment and Capitalist Form* (Cambridge, MA: Harvard University Press, 2020).

Amitava Kumar, who teaches at Vassar College, has published a lot. Each of his books seems to push against genre boundaries in different ways. On the short shelf of writing advice, his recent *Every Day I Write the Book: Notes on Style* deserves a place. As a writer, he's a teacher who doesn't offer pat answers. "Writing manuals ask you to 'find your voice.' But what does that mean? Better to start with something smaller and more concrete: 'Find your topic.'"[6]

I admire and share his bewilderment. Find your topic, yes, but then ask questions about it. Think about those questions and what they might mean for your readers.

As to the voice question, I'm not so sure writers *find* it, exactly. I'm more inclined to think that the writer has a gut feeling about ways in which something might be said, then thinks through how that gut feeling might play out within the constraints of a genre. If that's right, then writing is as much about *making* your voice as it is about finding it.

Still, we can make some useful distinctions among types of academic writing and the different voices we deploy.[7] Scholarly writing works in tight circles. Imagine you're giving a paper at a sociolinguistics conference on the contending messages of "Black Lives Matter" and "All Lives Matter." Your talk doesn't ask whether the messages overlap or stand in conflict. Instead you're exploring the socioeconomic

6. "Voice," in *Every Day I Write the Book* (Durham, NC: Duke University Press, 2020), Kindle edition. Kumar writes that his book's task is "to consider academic writing that is difficult to categorize, is challenging in a new way, or is noteworthy for its inventiveness" (part V, fn. 11).

7. T. S. Eliot's working title for what became *The Waste Land* was *He Do the Police in Different Voices*, a phrase plucked from Dickens's *Our Mutual Friend*. In that novel, the character of Sloppy is, we are told, "a beautiful reader of the newspaper, He do the Police in different voices." Reading one's own draft with different voices might be a tool for hearing shifts in the relationship you build between your writing and your readers.

conditions that determine what people *think they hear* in the two credos.

As you prepare your conference talk, you calibrate your analysis on the assumption that professional social linguists share common tools. Those tools both enable them to follow your scholarly oral presentation and allow you to get into the subject in as much technical detail as you want. You have a community of listeners who share a knowledge base and a set of interpretative skills. Your conference paper voice is calibrated for a conference audience.

Six months after your successful conference talk, you plan to submit it to a linguistics journal. You can develop even more fully the nuance of your argument and provide the relevant documentation. In doing that, you will depend on slow and careful reading by fellow professionals.

Only inexperienced speakers ignore the difference between a text to be heard and a text to be read. The earlier, oral presentation required a particular structure and texture: fewer dependent clauses, shorter sentences, perhaps a degree of spoken emphasis. The reader of a journal can, by contrast, sustain long, complex sentences. The writer can visually direct the reader's attention (with italics, boldface, the indentation of a new paragraph) in a way that can't be done at the podium.[8] And most importantly, you can add footnotes, deepen your argument, take positions on secondary features of your argument.

8. PowerPoint, which may have done more to alter public speaking than anything since the invention of the microphone, hasn't served speakers or audiences well. I'd argue that the benefits of PowerPoint's electronic display are easily offset by the poor public speaking skills the technology has fostered. Yes, use images when you speak but never as a substitute for your own embodied voice. PowerPoint is a convenient assistant but a terrible speaker.

But what if your next move after the oral presentation at a specialized meeting is not to a written presentation at a specialized journal? What happens when you try to reach a different, nonspecialized audience?

Your conference presentation is a hit, and you're encouraged to write it up for a *New York Times* op-ed. What will change from the conference delivery to the op-ed page? Overall length will be drastically reduced. Sentence-level complexity will be cooled. You'll be newly attentive to the visual shape of your text. You will work hard to hear the language you've chosen to present your ideas, this time for a readership that doesn't want technical arguments. Suddenly you're writing from your authority as a sociolinguist on a topic that speaks with urgency to the world, not just a seminar room full of specialist peers.

The op-ed piece catches the eye of a publisher, who offers you a contract for a trade book. Some nice money, a short deadline, plans for a media campaign. The book will need more of everything, including argument and context. But you'll nonetheless need to voice it the way you voiced the op-ed, retaining the quality that caught the publisher's eye.

Or was it the publisher's ear? If you're writing caught fire, was it the content alone or the way you presented it? How did you manage the balancing act of professional authority and human, even popular, appeal?

If you're fortunate to work with a good editor, you may enjoy the benefits of a hard, professional reading, in addition to outside specialist evaluations. Good readers, either in-house or outside, will be attuned not only to content and argument but also to voice. If you're working with an editor or readers' reports, you will inevitably revise; as you revise, work hard to hear your voice, not just your message.

THE QUESTION OF JARGON

We haven't looked at the vexed question of jargon, and we're not going to dwell on it for long here. Jargon and cliché are often linked: the obscurantist (intentionally difficult) and the banal (unintentionally vacant). A broom for sweeping the chimney of your writing would get rid of clichés (you may not say things like "easy as pie" these days, but "it is what it is" has achieved cliché status). Jargon is more complicated.

People have strong feelings about jargon, and it seems they always have. The fourteenth century was already on to the term as a marker of meaninglessness. Chaucer uses the word to refer to what the *OED* defines as "the inarticulate utterance of birds, or a vocal sound resembling it." (Inarticulate to us, maybe, though birds surely don't see it that way.)

In most fields, there is necessarily technical language. You might try to sidestep the charge of jargon by claiming a right to what are sometimes called "terms of art."[9] That's a tricky move. Terms of art are expressions that are intelligible within a given profession or field but not necessarily beyond the garden gate. Is this just another clubby inside-baseball language? Consider an invented example (invented in that I've changed names): "At the annual meeting, vice-chair Smith praised the division for right-sizing the sales team."[10] So what should a writer do about jargon? Does it help you reach an audience, or does it throw up a blockade?

9. On the scholar's conflicted relationship to jargon, see Marjorie Garber, *Academic Instincts* (Princeton, NJ: Princeton University Press, 2001).

10. "'Business model' is one of those terms of art that were central to the Internet boom." That usage example in the *OED*'s entry for "art" (definition 10c) cites Michael Lewis's *The New New Thing: A Silicon Valley Story* (New York: Norton, 2000). Of course, Theodor Adorno warned us of the "jargon of authenticity," but we don't seem to have listened.

Here a bit of social science terminology might help us out: endogenous features are those within a system, exogenous features are external to a system. So there's jargon that's internal to you and your group, which we might describe as endogenous, and there's jargon external to you and your group, which we could think of as exogenous. The group is your readership. Do you use words like *dialogic* and *teleological*? (I'm giving you gentle examples.) If you do and nobody flinches, you've just used endogenous jargon. You're talking inside-baseball, but everyone's on the same page. But if you use the same words in a different context—a popular magazine article about Native American foodways, for example—there's a good chance you'll have brought exogenous jargon to the table.

Beauty is in the eye of the beholder (yes, that's a cliché). Or, in other words, jargon is in the ear and discursive assumptions of the receptor (yes, that's pretty jargony).

So is jargon bad? That depends. Every day, we encounter unfamiliar, technical language. It would be difficult if not impossible to communicate complex ideas without access to at least some specialized terminology. When we call it jargon, we're really saying that it's exogenous, meaning we don't like it because it sounds unnecessarily complex, or mysterious, or pretentious. Or simply that the presence of that specialized language draws a line in the sand separating the alienated reader from the comfortable one.

When jargon is appropriately used, it does necessary specialized work for the right readership. If you think of jargon, or any specialized language, as a set of tools, to be used cautiously but whenever necessary, you'll be on the right track. Use the language of your discipline as you need it, but calibrate that need to your audience. No one can tell you how much technical language is right for what you're writing. No one can tell you what words to use or what tone of voice will guarantee writerly success, however that could be measured. And no one can tell you what familiar or uncategorizable shape will do what you want to make your writing work.

What we're calling "voice" is part of the calibration that William Zinsser calls taste. And taste, he declares,

> is a mixture of qualities that are beyond analyzing: an ear that can hear the difference between a sentence that limps and a sentence that lilts, an intuition that knows when a casual or vernacular phrase dropped into a formal sentence will not only sound right but will seem to be the inevitable choice.[11]

Taste, he tells us, is something you're born with or you're not, though even if you're not, you can learn something, chiefly by studying other writers who have a skill you're still in need of developing. Zinsser sets our eyes squarely on writing models: read the best writers in your field and beyond, listen for how they craft a sentence, a paragraph, the smoothness that joins section to section to section.

Like Anne Lamott, Zinsser has an appealing, conversational style. He writes as if he were teaching a class to aspiring journalists, eager to sell their stories in periodicals. And like Lamott, he encourages you to write what you know, what you're excited by, and who you are.

These are valuable lessons about writing (and, yes, life, too), but they don't always translate easily into the more

11. *On Writing Well: The Classic Guide to Writing Nonfiction*, 30th anniversary ed. (New York: Harper Perennial, 2006), Kindle page 166.

formal systems of scholarly research and academic critique. If no writer on writing can tell you precisely how long your sentences should be, much less what needs to be in them, you won't find a handy guide that tells you how much of your own experience, your own identity, your struggle belongs in what you're writing. You'll have to calibrate that for yourself.[12]

Helen Sword has cheerfully made bad academic writing the target of her research. Her ear for jargon is tuned to the broadest frequency across the humanities and the social sciences. *Stylish Academic Writing* sets out to free scholarly writers from the self-harm of so much academic prose. Being "stylish" means many things, including developing a feel for one's self as present on the page, speaking as an educated writer to other, educated readers. Jargon is something to be escaped, and *Stylish Academic Writing* is all about giving the writer courage.[13]

Where to find that courage? If you've been heartened by what you've read so far, you'll know that I'm going to lead you back to your own text. When in doubt about jargon, you can look more closely at your keywords. If your draft depends on a set of technical concepts, embrace that. Watering down precise but difficult terms won't guarantee that you'll be able to use them to the same effect. If you're going to use technical language, use it. Just remember that an audience will either know that language or need to have it explained.

12. If this sounds as if the question of audience has been momentarily turned around—the thing you're writing is suddenly pointing not at them out there but back at you—that's OK. Writing secret: you're part of the audience for whom you write.
13. *Stylish Academic Writing* (Cambridge, MA: Harvard University Press, 2012).

THE VOICES OF OTHERS

"Siri, how do I revise my manuscript?"

"I'm sorry, I can't answer that. Have you tried asking Alexa?"

Voice-enabled technology connects the human voice to computer programming, translating your human words into information and information back into sounds that convincingly resemble the human voice.

Writers spend their whole lives doing the same thing.

The writer has a voice, a human voice that gets recreated, transformed, rebuilt in written language. It's funny how we can say things in writing we wouldn't say out loud, and vice versa. Writing is a speech-enabled technology. Fictional characters who tell us their own stories are voice-enabled inventions. Brontë's Jane Eyre, Salinger's Holden Caulfield, and Ellison's Invisible Man are given the power of speech by the writers who are in control of the proceedings. Poetry is all about voice (it's about a lot else, too). Or think of a contemporary novel like Chiminanda Ngozi Adichie's *Americanah*. Adichie knows the art of dialogue and delivery, switching up scenes, shaping a story and keeping the information coming for the reader. That kind of writerly skill is hard to imagine without an effective writing voice.

Voice is critical to trade nonfiction, too. In *Tightrope*, Nicholas Kristof and Sheryl WuDunn analyze the economic plight of individuals who the subtitle identifies as "Americans Reaching for Hope." It's a book about people who haven't made it in a country that values making it above everything else.

No, that's not right. *Tightrope* is a harrowing account of the great number of Americans who are ignored by those who can afford to ignore them. It's about drugs and alcohol, about rape and poverty, and about being the invisible citizens for whom politicians' promises are just that. We might say, in narrative terms, that those politicians' words are empty because they have rhetoric but not voice. When they talk to the press, the art of public speaking is soullessly demonstrated, the smile always camera-ready. Then the cameras are shut off, but people's lives don't change for the better. Like the ethnographies to which it bears a sibling relationship, *Tightrope* aims to give voice to those whose voices haven't been heard.

Adichie and Kristof and WuDunn have written bestsellers. That's an unlikely outcome for most of us. Yet academic writing shares with the novelist and with the investigative economist a commitment to voice *as a responsibility*.

But responsibility to whom or to what?

A writer, especially a writer of nonfiction, takes on responsibility to a subject. Tell the truth about your ideas. Find language that lets you communicate those ideas. That's your responsibility to your own voice. Tell the truth about your subject. That's your responsibility to the world.

So how do other voices work? Adichie creates characters, listens to them as she imagines them speaking, and does what a novelist has to do: be true to the voices of her creations. Kristof and WuDunn take as their responsibility listening to and communicating to readers the voices of the people they write about. Art and the social sciences may have more in common than we think.

How does this work in more specialized academic writing? If you're quoting, whether a secondary or a primary source, you're not just citing to support a point: you're calling up someone else's voice. Listen to those voices and tell the truth of what you hear.

You're also juxtaposing those voices with your own. In the social sciences, it can be too easy to construct a proposal or research plan that summarizes fieldwork without making space to quote the words of the surveyed or interviewed. It can be tempting to let analyses overwhelm, and sometimes erase, the first-person voice of the writer's research subjects. People you talk to for your research share their voices with you. Share those voices with others.[14]

But quoting too much can obscure or drown out your own ideas. Quoting too much text that's beautifully written might make your own writing feel a little less brilliant. Getting the balance of quoted material to your own words is partly about keeping voices in balance. Revising for audience includes being sure that you're the center of your own work while not hogging the microphone.

Take the measure of your field, and be brave. Readers, including publishers, love to hear the voices of real people. Remember that those real voices were probably what got you interested in your topic to begin with. Why not share that excitement? Aim for a balance between what you and fellow scholars have to say, but make space for other voices. Remember, too, that you've asked them to speak with you because they know things you don't.

Voice in writing is finally less about speaking than about giving. Give your readers what makes it possible for them to engage your ideas. Be generous. Make whatever you're writing an opportunity for your reader, not simply an obligation, either for you or for them.

Do this and you'll like your own writing more, too.

---

14. Just be sure to anonymize your subjects or get permission to quote.

7

What writing wants

The only writing that counts is the writing that you've taken to its necessary final form. Sometime, somewhere, there's a writer—a professor or a journalist, a historian or graduate student in education, a staff writer or a grants officer—who will be asked the question, "And what do you do for a living?" The writer will smile and say, "I revise."

Writing is one thing, but rewriting is the real, messy thing.

As Howard Becker puts it with refreshing directness, "Rewriting destroys your neatness." The work of writing means cross-outs, holes, gaps, on the page and in your thinking. "You find that a thought that doesn't belong where you put it works better somewhere else."[1] That's not all revision means, but it's a lot of it. If revision isn't messy, you're not doing it right. And still, you've got to finish it, make it presentable for others.

1. *Writing for Social Scientists*, 3rd ed. (Chicago: University of Chicago Press, 2020), 154.

COHESION AND PERSISTENCE

I've asked many people how they revise, what their practical tips are, how they go about getting beyond the blank page or the brick wall of a recalcitrant draft, how they figure out when they're done. Few put forward methodical advice that others could follow. And yet I know that they've found ways forward for themselves, as the evidence of their writing makes clear. They've found something to say, pulled it together well, tied it up for the reader. Tied, but not too tightly.

Revision aims to tie a piece of writing together. To make it coherent. Meaning what, exactly? When language, structure, tone, and genre expectations are all in alignment, we say that a piece of writing is coherent. The piece isn't self-contradicting. No funny bits stick out. It makes sense as a whole. Its parts cohere. It will not fall apart when you pick it up.

But how to pull everything together so that that's the effect? On good days, the well-designed writing project can seem to move on its own. It's not that the writing automatically appears on the page, but sometimes what you're working on feels as if it, and not you, knows what has to happen next. That's the exhilarating, and maybe uncanny, feeling of being at the keyboard and not wanting to break your concentration. Not because you're aware that you're making stuff up right there at the computer, but because it feels as if the writing knows where it wants to go and what it wants to do. At moments like that, it's as if you the writer are needed to be sure it goes there. Seize those moments. Treasure them.

A rational reader of the previous paragraph will say that

I'm mistaking the mental labor of writing for those sporadic moments when the prose comes faster than I might have expected. I warned you early on that thinking about revision can lead to thinking of the writing as having its own destination and its own will. But of course it's really the clarity of the argument and the persuasiveness of the structure that largely determine the coherence of a rewrite.

For most of us, rearranging a stretch of writing leaves gaps. In writing, there can be big cracks where the draft bottoms out and the reader is expected not to notice. (The reader will notice.) A good rereading should send up danger signs right away. Big cracks in your writing will be easy to hear and easy to see.

I need a footnote here.
This moves too fast.
Um, isn't this paragraph contradicting what I said earlier?

There are other kinds of cracks, too. The slippages between paragraphs, for example. Listen to the movement from one paragraph to the next. Every paragraph is its own little drama, with a beginning and an end. That's how you know it's a paragraph.

Shaping a paragraph, then, is making a paragraph happen. Have something to say, but don't forget to apply linking words and phrases that will make it easier for your reader to hear your ideas. *Nevertheless, . . . Given these conditions, . . . As if to prove the point, . . .* You will have your own repertoire. These are transitions and hooks. Each gives a clear indication of the relation of the current paragraph to the preceding one.

Poor transitions are like bad sticky tape. If you've written an ironic sentence that begins "Also," (that's *also, comma*) go back and figure out what you meant. Avoid cheap connectors. Give your reader something to work with.[2]

Don't be afraid of the sentence fragment. It's not a mortal writing sin. Only a stern, inner writing coach would require you to eliminate every SFRAG in your draft.[3] In fact, a cheeky fragment is sometimes exactly what you want.

Getting to that coherence, though, can be messy and time-consuming, and experienced writers have learned to anticipate revision's workload. If you're gifted with an especially powerful sense of your writing objectives, you may need to spend less time thinking through the strategies behind effective revision. (If that's you, the work of revising may come naturally.) For other writers, the shape and point of the thing being written will only cohere over time, and only by means of multiple attempts to get the ideas down in words.

I rewrite a lot, not only books like this, which I hope might be of interest to many kinds of readers, but specialized academic writing, which I know will only be of interest to small readerships. I try to begin a writing day by reviewing what I've written or revised the day before. Not exactly like a film director screening rushes, but at least a bit like that.

Whenever I can, I read out my drafts out loud. I make comments in the margin, sometimes asking myself what I mean, sometimes wondering if this paragraph should go earlier or later. I delete a lot, though I hold the deleted passages in suspension. I don't want to throw anything out. At least not yet. I might change my mind, I tell myself. (I seem to be always

2. More than one weakly structured manuscript feels as if it should be entitled "Oh, and One More Thing."
3. Clearly, I'm not that inner writing coach. Yes, students need to know why sentence fragments are problematic. Since you do, use them effectively. And start a sentence with "and" if you want to.

wrong about this. Only rarely do I put back something I've cut. Why? Because there is an endless number of ways to say something, which means that the odds of saying it better are very, very high.) I add new words, tentatively, as suggestions. I go through again, listening to the additions one more time. Reject, accept, or relocate: with every potential addition, I seem to want to make a decision right away. Potential cuts, however, can linger in writing limbo a bit longer. Sometimes for weeks.

In my morning rereads, I often have a general feeling that the individual sentences look fine but that they may not connect easily enough for a reader who isn't me. So I tweak by inserting little sentences or clauses, little bursts of words.

Let me explain that again.
A paradox? Maybe not.
This doesn't disqualify X, but it gives X a new context.
Let's recap.
Never? Well, hardly ever.
That's the standard interpretation of the data.

These short spurts don't make claims as much as they let in some air for the reader to breathe before plunging back into a serious stretch of argument, letting the reader linger just long enough on a strong point, spend just enough time on a less important one, and then move to another idea. A musician might say that they're there to fill out the phrase.

A friend told me these were stool softeners, which seemed a bit cruel. But at least I was reminded of what *Bird by Bird*'s Anne Lamott calls her "shitty drafts," those necessary, terrible-but-at-least-I've-got-something-down first versions out of which much better things will emerge. These little interstitial moments, bits of writerly grout, can let in some light and a bit of writing personality, too, and contribute to the quality many writers mean by voice. Thinking about transitions and coherence inevitably jumbles up argument, architecture, and audience; you knew that would happen.

Transitions can be big or small, loud or whisper-quiet. For some writers, the care in transition makes the writing gossamer, subtly shifting from one moment to the next. That's more likely for a brilliant essayist, novelist, or poet than for a scholarly writer (we have hard jobs thinking about hard problems, plus we need footnotes). But if you can read your draft article in terms of music or quantitative verse, thinking in long stretches and short, emphatic moments and bits that flesh out the emphases, you'll be able to hear what your reader will hear.

Are there enigmas as tantalizing as "continuity"? Alfred Hitchcock's 1948 thriller *Rope*, long famous for seeming to be shot in one continuous take, actually has ten cuts, some cleverly hidden, where the camera needed to change reels.[4] You will still hear it described casually as the Hitchcock film that was shot in one room and as one continuous scene. With a different, digital camera, the 2002 film *Russian Ark*, directed by Aleksandr Sokurov, manages to do what *Rope* seems to, and on a far grander scale. Journeying through history and thirty-three rooms of St. Petersburg's Hermitage Museum, that film is miraculously one continuous shot.

If you're writing like a film director, or better still a film editor, you're calculating where a camera needs to be and for how long. Writing does similar things, except with words.[5]

4. Film editor Vashi Nedomansky, ACE, explains the cuts in his blog, https://vashivisuals.com/alfred-hitchcock-hiding-cuts-rope/.
5. Of course, a film commands its own temporality. A text can't exact the same demands from its readers.

Are you a writer who aims for the illusion of seamlessness? Maybe. But if you're like most scholars, you might prefer meaningful breaks, redirections, asides, ruptures. However you approach the question of coherence, you want all the parts of your writing to stick to one another in some way that's meaningful to you so that your reader will perceive what you've written as purposeful.

There are other kinds of writerly stickiness, too. You want your ideas to stick with your reader. You want your insights and theories to be substantial, satisfying. Nourishing the way you might still hear someone say of a hearty meal that it sticks to your ribs. Arguments and structures convey your ideas, while voice and a sensitivity to your audience make that nourishing meal appetizing for hungry minds. If readers have picked up your essay or article or book, they're hungry. So feed them well.

In the world of digital business, which is to say the world of social media, stickiness is the durability of a product or a concept, measured by the number and frequency of visitors to a site. If you write a blog or aspire to being an Instagram mogul, or even if you're simply trying to drum up and sustain interest in a project or campaign, you want people to come to your site, again and again. You want, in other words, as much of their divided attention as you can capture. Stickiness is a good thing.

You also want to stick the landing, to be that inner gymnast hurtling through a routine and finishing up exactly where you want to end. (Feet firm on the mat, arms stretched back, smile beaming. Or the academic's equivalent.) You'll know when the piece has landed. It's the sweetest feeling a writer can have.

THE SPEED OF THOUGHT

The right kind of stickiness is important, but so is pace. Good writing, like a good movie or a good play, is well paced. Pace isn't speed. A good swimmer manages a 1600-meter freestyle race through skill and strategy, which includes timing and pace, not simply speed. Musicians strategize, too, though they do it cooperatively, not competitively. And writers?

A theme of this book has been that the best writing is cooperative; the writer and the reader are a bit like instruments playing together, if in different spaces, and maybe years apart.[6] The writer can, of course, control only so much of the relationship, but that so much can be quite a lot.

In scholarly writing, pacing is the element of prose that controls the velocity and frequency with which information and ideas are delivered to the reader. Some writers don't think about pace at all, presumably because they're working so hard on making a case and proving their argument. The examples that you line up and analyze are there to bring new information to the reader and to bring the reader closer to your perspective on the problem you're addressing. Argument and evidence are, of course, critical to the writer's task. But pace might be even more to the point.

Here's a writing exercise: read over your draft. Mark it up with two indicators. Just a plus and a minus sign are enough to note where the writing is fast and where it's slow. Now look at those textual moments. Are they fast where you want

6. The coronavirus pandemic has brought into our homes the digital intimacy of musicians who are playing instruments in isolation but whose separated sounds can be coordinated into music. There's something extraordinarily moving about watching a singer in one country and a pianist in another collaborating to perform through digital space. There might even be a model here for thinking about you and your reader.

them to be fast? Where you want to speed the reader along? Are they slower and more deliberate where the writing needs more exacting attention from your reader?

Sometimes fast is exactly what you need: the hairpin turn, the surprise, the shocking assertion. Sometimes slow is necessary: you're working out (slowly, slower) the details of your analysis, you need to rehearse the historical conditions of a situation, you want to catalogue a line of approaches that you will now—fast, faster—unsettle, preparing your reader for your own insights.

If this feels dramatic, it's meant to be. Writing isn't unrelated to the theater. In fact, Western culture has found a point of relation between the theater and pretty much everything else. *Theatrum mundi* (the theater of the world, the world as theater) is what people in literature call a trope. Writing is its own little theater, and the writer, both playwright and director. A good director knows how to pace what the playwright has crafted. Good actors know how to pace what they've been given to do. Writers pace, too, and as with theater, we often don't notice the skill in pacing because the play, or the novel, or the scholarly work, so completely holds our attention.

Parts and whole, big and little, major and minor, slow and fast, complex and straightforward. Boring writing settles for one in each pair. One writer writes in a monotone, making one minor point slowly and with great complexity. Another writer presents a great big, fast, straightforward, collection of little pieces, each of which the writer thinks is urgent. Neither sounds like an ideal model. You can bore a reader by being slow and tedious, but you can also confuse and alienate a reader by tossing out ideas helter-skelter, insisting that everything is equally important.

Make choices. Change it up. Repeat with variation. Be

present in your writing. Don't worry that you'll be letting your guard down, much less letting your team down, if you let yourself take part in what you're writing. You will take part, in any case. The choice is to do it either passively and with reluctance, or intentionally and with presence.[7]

In writing, presence isn't saying, "Look at me!" It's taking control of the way you say what you have to say. Beyond transitions, which are necessarily everywhere in a piece of written work, three elements of your writing need special attention. Give your text its last run-through and focus on these: the opening, the climactic points, and the close.

What's a climactic point for an academic writer? Maybe the moment where one last strong piece of evidence powerfully confirms your subtly presented argument. Maybe it's a big reveal (thank you, architects). Or maybe there will be several climactic moments, one in each part of what you're assembling. Chapters, which need to be semi-autonomous, will each require some sort of climactic point, even if it's as straightforward and unfancy as saying, "The point is that *all* participants in this study were deliberately made unaware of" whatever it might be.

A reader is entitled to know what the writer thinks is important. It's never enough to say, "Well, if the reader didn't understand, then I suggest rereading more carefully." I warned you about baby phenomenology. It's the writer's job to make the reader eager to read and, if necessary, reread. Be sure you've constructed your chapter, or essay, or magnum opus so that the reader knows what you think is important. The longer your text, the more transitions and climactic points you may have, but the principle remains the same.

All of these writing elements have a temporality. You can

7. This is part of what Helen Sword means by "stylish" writing.

speed up or slow down your audience's reading speed by making sentences longer and more complex or short and pithy. Pacing is as much a component of style as word choice or a taste for metaphor. This writerly power is quite independent of the content of those sentences.

Within that flow there are moments you want your reader to remember. They're the important points, the bits that a book review might quote at length or a blogger might find and make globally available. A last rereading is done with your ears, listening in particular to the wording of your most important points. Or do what a reviewer might do: reread your draft and isolate a half-dozen sentences that seem the most likely to be quoted, argued over, or reported through social media. "But what about the context?" you'll ask. Yes, of course, the points you've made only make complete sense within the larger picture. But that's often not how writers are quoted. How do these six sentences read out of context? Can the smallest adjustment now reduce the chance of being misinterpreted later?

STOP SIGNS

Dutiful readers, bless them, make it all the way to the last page, which is where the reader's sidewalk ends. Academic writing rarely takes the time to stop when it needs to. Scholars rarely leave the reader wanting more.

Which is a pity. Knowing your manuscript is knowing where to stop. In Victorian times, a signature might be underscored with an elaborate pen squiggle. It's called a paraph (figure 7.1). Charles Dickens loved to sign his name with them.

You're probably not going to sign off on a book manuscript with a big, inky paraph or even a bold line across the last

7.1 Charles Dickens's autograph (1838). Photograph: Wikimedia Commons.

sentence you type out, but somehow you want to signal, to yourself and to your readers, that you've reached the end and this is where it stops.

Never stop *because* you run out of things to say. Of course, if you have run out of things to say, call a halt. But then immediately go back and read what you've written. Dead ends and freezes are a sign that you haven't quite worked a problem out. Better to stop when and because you've said as best you can what you wanted to communicate. If you've done that well, you might have more that you *could* say, but you won't, because you're writing intentionally, economically, with an eye to persuasion. A friend once reduced an academic audience to knowing laughter by beginning a talk with the words, "In the shorter version of this paper, I . . ." The joke, of course, inverted the standard conference presentation's opening apology, "In the longer version of this paper," a phrase meant to alert the audience to the existence of a longer, more coherent version of the talk than the one the speaker is about to deliver.[8]

If you say everything you know about something, you've said too much. Among the dangers of academic writing is not knowing where the off-ramp lies. Each of us needs to

8. The talk by Andrew Parker was a piece of the thinking that went into his book on critical theory and the maternal, *The Theorist's Mother* (Durham, NC: Duke University Press, 2012). But what I remember most from the talk is his verbal gesture and the audience's reading of it.

be cautious not to overstay our writerly welcome. Our arguments and crucial observations will be more effective if we don't pad them out with unnecessary variations on an argumentative theme.

The ending, if it is an ending, needs to make logical or argumentative sense, but it's even more important as an opportunity. It's the last thing a reader encounters, the last thing the author presents. It could be a summary statement, a provocation, a stepping forward, a stepping back. Whatever you have to say, this is your last chance to reflect or reinforce. Don't waste it. Avoid *thus*. Hold the spotlight for a few seconds. Then get off the stage.

Back in the discussion of architecture, I suggested the slightly counterintuitive model of a **W**, a writing trajectory that moved from first statement to conclusion, then to developmental middle, before revisiting the end and, finally, returning to the beginning. I would be untrue to my premise if I didn't end this long meditation on revising writing where I advise you to: with page 1. *How* you end is likely to be the last thing your reader will hear. But the last act of revising should take you to the beginning of your text. Ask yourself these questions:

> *Does your opening do the work you need it to?*
> *Does it seize the opportunity to put the reader smack into the*
>   *problem you're exploring?*
> *Does it situate the reader?*
> *Does it undo expectations?*
> *Does it establish tone and approach, and subtly build confidence*
>   *in doing so?*

There are lots of ways to make a first sentence work. Your first sentence might name your subject, or your problem, or your fight. It will almost certainly identify your voice and the genre of the writing to follow. Make your opening reach for something. The only "wrong" opening is one that doesn't reach at all.

Most of us have favorite first sentences. (For this exercise, novels don't count, not even *Pride and Prejudice*.) Think of great openers in nonfiction and even in scholarly tomes. An example I turn to frequently comes from historian of science Steven Shapin. It's the opener of his book *The Scientific Revolution*: "There was no such thing as the Scientific Revolution, and this is a history of it."

Boom. And we're off. What a great sentence! It's got voice, economy, focus. The book that follows that opener puts under pressure the validity of a phrase that has long been used as a historical and epistemological marker. Shapin's study takes the subject of seventeenth-century science and uses it to think through how we make assumptions about knowledge and pass those assumptions on. Can you imagine a first sentence of your own draft that aims for that energy and elan? Nothing about Shapin's sixteen-word salvo suggests that the book will be circling around a subject in order to find a protected nook, like a bird circling a rooftop at dusk.

But I see we're back to birds again. As I'm writing this page, the birds outside my window are making their short, sunset flights, stopping briefly on a landing or a rooftop, then flying off again to wherever birds go. A slightly perverse thought at the end of a book about writing, but if you bear with me, I hope you'll take it in the positive spirit in which it's meant. In *The Miracle of Analogy*, the theorist and visual studies scholar Kaja Silverman formulates a brilliant cut through the history of our thinking about the photographic image. Silverman argues that photography is "the world's primary way of revealing itself to us."[9] Her project is to understand how pictures work: the relation between the concrete, instant-bound photograph and the thing in the world that it *represents*. How is a photograph of something in the world different from the thing itself? The "miracle" at the heart of that relationship feels akin to the relation of writing to ideas. Writing is using words *as if* words and ideas and things could be mapped perfectly onto one another. We know that's not true. And still, when we revise, we work to repair, to improve, and to extend.

Writing is analogy. We write *about* things. But our writing is never the thing itself or even a copy of it. All writers, not just poets and novelists, are analogists. Everything we write is partial and angled (there's the Jacob metaphor again). It's all analogy, the broken mirror held up to the damaged, dysfunctional world we write to understand and maybe to heal. Why else write? What else to write about? Or with?

As you make your writing into a new version of itself, you'll give new shapes to your ideas. Revisions aren't just better versions of something, though if they aren't improvements they've failed in an important way. They're new forms, new bodies. You rethink your archives and put what you've found into new narrative shapes. Your obsessions and analogies will become questions you present as gifts.

In the eighteenth century, Benjamin Franklin penned his own epitaph. The inscription, now beloved of book historians, among others, famously plays out the idea of the

9. *The Miracle of Analogy, or The History of Photography, Part 1* (Stanford: Stanford University Press, 2015). In a conversation at Cooper Union with Walid Raad, Silverman paraphrased that insight: "photography is the world's way of showing us that it exists." Try to write at least one sentence like that in your own work.

human being as a published book and the resurrection as the Divine Author's revision of his earthly remains. The tattered volume of Franklin's body is destined through faith to appear once again "in a new and more elegant Edition / Corrected and improved / by the Author." That's Death as the last rewrite, and the Final Publisher, too.

In our own time, the American writer Nathaniel Mackey's "Song of the Andoumboulou," a poem about Black life, plays with ideas of creation. It's also about the author's own life, as he spent decades composing the poem. The unfamiliar term in the title is derived from Dogon culture, a mythic figure who is, in the author's words, "a failed form, a rough draft of humanity."

Mackey even talks about an idea of "Andoumboulouousness," which he glosses as "the idea that we're hopefully getting better, that we're a draft closer to what we mean when we say *humanity* in an idealistic sense." Improvement? Maybe, if we can think of it that way. But also the idea that Andoumboulouousness "is never satisfied with any of its iterations, that it will continue to go on and on and on."[10]

Writing and revision are human tasks. Tasks that humans do, tasks that are about humanity. Are they ever done? We write, we revise, we live out our own revisions. Unless we refuse to learn and slam the door shut, we learn and grow, and so we're changing all the time.

The jargon term "personal growth" points to psychological and ethical development, internal changes that are not necessarily written on the external body. Writing is different. All that changing happens at our desks or wherever we adjust

10. Nathaniel Mackey, "The Art of Poetry No. 107," *Paris Review*, no. 232 (Spring 2020).

our work in progress. Tinkering, rethinking, revising. Until it's as done as it's going to be.

When are you finished? How do you know? James Baldwin's view of revision is bracingly unsentimental. "It's very painful. You know it's finished when you can't do anything more to it, though it's never exactly the way you want it." Clearer, stronger, nearer, but not a perfect version. That's the challenge for all of us, each time we write, each time we revise.

In the end, the only version that counts is the last one you show the world, the last shape you make out of words, your text's last flight. Its layers and its histories, all the revisionist paths the final cut has taken to get where it is, they're now all part of what you do and know as a writer. Which is as it must be. But readers only see the writing you show them.

Make it the best you can, from page 1 through all the pages that follow.

Then let it go.

Acknowledgments

For helping me get this small book out into the world, some very big thanks are in order. Outside readers at the University of Chicago Press gave me important feedback and helped me keep in mind the necessity of two focal points: big picture, my reader; general, specific; large, small. These were not secrets, much less revelations. Like going to the eye doctor and having one's eyes checked for distance and close-up work, good revision has to look both far and near.[1]

When your text is recalcitrant, it helps to have a firm but patient editor, which is only one reason I'm fortunate to have the opportunity to work once again with Alan Thomas, friend, book meister, and editorial director at the University of Chicago Press, aided by the keen-eyed Randy Petilos, also a Press editor and friend. Better than anyone, Alan knows that this book has evolved over too many years. I hope it's not overcooked, because that's a danger with long-simmering, fitfully erupting projects. I tell myself that this book's ideas,

1. A few years back, I wrote a book called *Eye Chart*. As the title suggests, it's about how we see and how we developed a way of measuring that ability. Only now do I understand that it was a book about writing, sort of.

such as they are, have benefited from a long, slow marinade. Special thanks to Joel Score, senior manuscript editor at the Press, who patiently helped me keep my eye on what I was trying to say.

Many people have shared their thoughts with me about the subject of this book, which means people who have taught me more than they realize about writing. I couldn't possibly name them all here, but a few deserve to be marked as present in these pages. Over the past several years, I've spent long hours talking with my friend Kit Nicholls, director of the Center for Writing at Cooper Union, about teaching and about how students learn. We've recently cowritten a book on teaching called *Syllabus: The Remarkable, Unremarkable Document That Changes Everything* (Princeton University Press, 2020). I hope that *Syllabus* and *On Revision* share a sense of the importance of lived experience, whether that life belongs to writer or teacher, to student or reader.

I need to thank Pam Newton and John Lundberg at the Center for Writing, as well as to several brief generations of writing associates, who worked with me or with my Cooper Union students, and who allowed me to try to learn more and learn better about teaching this stuff. My time in publishing gave me invaluable opportunities to work with remarkable scholars who could write and think, and revise. There are too many to mention, but among them are Marjorie Garber, Kaja Silverman, and Eve Kosofsky Sedgwick, three scholars whose fleeting appearances in these pages fail to suggest what I have learned from their work. Nick Tampio counseled an author who felt blocked to scrap it all and start from the beginning, on the optimistic assumption that what was really important about my subject was already in my head and would find its way onto the page again, only this time in better form.

The biggest thanks are necessarily impossible. I've been fortunate over many years to talk to and with scholars and teachers (and scholar-teachers) at many conferences, colleges, and universities. Those invitations to speak and to lead workshops on writing and publishing became teaching experiences for me, and so learning experiences for thinking about why scholars write and how they can write "more effectively." I've put that phrase in quotation marks because it's so easily misunderstood as pointing to "outcomes" (or Outcomes™), a not unuseful concept that has unfortunately become the corporate university's flag. Sure, writing can have outcomes, but writing's about a lot more than that. Ideas, beliefs, imagination, risk, life. Those are just a few possibilities.

So my sincere gratitude to people who, over many years, have let me speak with them, their colleagues, students, and alumni, about a lot of things related to publishing, writing, editing, and how learning happens. Revision is never far from any of those things. Let me gratefully acknowledge here faculty, staff, program directors, and deans who made those visits possible. It's a long list, and I'm slightly embarrassed to trot it out here, but whatever is of value in this or any of my books owes a debt to the people I've learned from. Seminars, workshops, and lecture halls have made me welcome at the University of Otago and the University of Sydney in one part of the globe, and in another the European universities of Oslo, Stockholm, Uppsala, and Amsterdam, the Blekinge Institute of Technology, the University of Bern, ETH Zurich, and Pompeu Fabra University in Barcelona.

In North America, let me record thanks to the universities of California (Davis, Berkeley, Santa Cruz, Santa Barbara, Los Angeles, and Irvine), Chicago, Florida, Hawaii, Idaho, Illinois at Chicago, Louisiana, Maryland (College Park),

Massachusetts (Boston), Miami, Michigan, Missouri, Nebraska, North Carolina (Wilmington), Pennsylvania, Texas (Austin), Toronto, Southern California, Vermont, Virginia, and Washington, as well as institutions that don't begin with "university of," including Arizona State, Barnard, Bucknell, Case Western, Connecticut College, CUNY (the Graduate Center and CCNY), Emory, Fairleigh Dickinson, Florida State, Gettysburg, Hamilton, Harvard, Loyola (Chicago) and Loyola (New Orleans), Louisiana State, Middlebury, NYU (Washington Square and Abu Dhabi), Ohio State, Princeton, Rutgers, SUNY at Farmingdale, Union, Vanderbilt, Stanford, and my almae matres, Columbia and Indiana (Bloomington).

I also need to thank the Association of University Presses, the Ford Foundation Fellows Program, and the Modern Language Association for opportunities to think out loud, with others, about what writing and revision is and does. Special thanks to the teachers and editors who took part in two terrific MLA sessions I had the good fortune to organize: the first at the 2007 Annual Meeting on "Writing as Revision, Revision as Writing," with David Bartholomae, Cathy Birkenstein-Graff, Susan Gubar, Bill Regier, and Jeff Williams; and the second in 2017 on the same topic, with Greg Britton, Sam Cohen, Sharon Marcus, and Ayanna Thompson. In retrospect, I can see that this book began after that first session and got the necessary reboot after the second.

Let me also thank here all the editors I've worked with over the years: Penny Kaiserlian, Paul Schellinger, and Linda Halvorson at Chicago; Peter Dougherty at Princeton; Rebecca Barden at the British Film Institute; and Haaris Naqvi, as well as Object Lessons series editors Ian Bogost and Chris Schaberg, at Bloomsbury. What they helped me see in my earlier books has inevitably shaped these pages. Ditto to many colleagues in publishing and teaching, as well as hundreds of casual and close friends at the MLA and the Shakespeare Association of America, a list of whom would be too long for comfort, so their names will remain *in pectore*. In short, everyone who has said to me, "A book about revising writing? *We so need that!*" has kept me plugging long.

For about five years, I wrote a biweekly column on language for the *Chronicle of Higher Education* as part of its *Lingua Franca* blog. You can learn a lot about revising from working on a short stretch of text, repeatedly, under deadline. I'll take this moment to thank Liz McMillen and Heidi Landecker of the *CHE* for the chance to write (and rewrite, and rewrite, and rewrite) those journalistic bagatelles, little essays about words and what we do with and to them, as well as about what words do with and to us.

With her customary flair and enthusiasm, my agent Tanya McKinnon of McKinnon Literary guided this book once again to the University of Chicago Press.

Special thanks to the Morgan Library for permission to reproduce the Balzac proof page.

Now and always again, I thank my students, even the ones for whom writing is visibly a struggle. Teaching and learning aren't even on a continuum; they're one thing.

Of course, thanks (wrong word) to Diane Gibbons, my always-partner in this great adventure, who has endured yet one more extended chunk of our lives occupied with my trying to solve the problem of writing a book. I say this every time I publish something. It's always true.

That's enough about how these pages happened. Let *On Revision* help you follow—and lead, and follow—your own writing to the place it needs to be.

You can do it. Just keep your ears open.

A very short bibliography

Baldwin, James. "The Art of Fiction No. 78." *Paris Review*, no. 91
 (Spring 1984). https://www.theparisreview.org/interviews
 /2994/james-baldwin-the-art-of-fiction-no-78-james-baldwin
Becker, Howard. *Writing for Social Scientists*. 3rd edition.
 Chicago: University of Chicago Press, 2020.
Belcher, Wendy. *Writing Your Journal Article in Twelve Weeks:
 A Guide to Academic Publishing Success*. 2nd edition. Chicago:
 University of Chicago Press, 2019.
Booth, Wayne, and Greg Colomb. *The Craft of Research*. 4th
 edition. Chicago: University of Chicago Press, 2016.
Garber, Marjorie. *Academic Instincts*. Princeton, NJ: Princeton
 University Press, 2001.
Germano, William. *From Dissertation to Book*. 2nd edition.
 Chicago: University of Chicago Press, 2013.
Germano, William. *Getting It Published: A Guide for Scholars and
 Anyone Else Serious about Serious Books*. 3rd edition. Chicago:
 University of Chicago Press, 2016.
Germano, William, and Kit Nicholls. *Syllabus: The Remarkable,
 Unremarkable Document That Changes Everything*. Princeton,
 NJ: Princeton University Press 2020.

Ghodsee, Kristen. *From Notes to Narrative: Writing Ethnographies That Everyone Can Read*. Chicago: University of Chicago Press, 2016.

Gooblar, David. *The Missing Course: Everything They Never Taught You about College Teaching*. Cambridge, MA: Harvard University Press, 2019.

Graff, Gerald, and Cathy Birkenstein. *They Say/I Say: The Moves That Matter in Academic Writing*. 4th edition. New York: W. W. Norton, 2018.

Haag, Pamela. *Revise: The Scholar-Writer's Essential Guide to Tweaking, Editing, and Perfecting Your Manuscript*. New Haven, CT: Yale University Press, 2021.

Kahneman, Daniel. *Thinking, Fast and Slow*. New York: Farrar, Straus and Giroux, 2011.

Kumar, Amitava. *Every Day I Write the Book: Notes on Style*. Durham, NC: Duke University Press, 2020.

Lamott, Anne. *Bird by Bird: Instructions for Writing and Life*. New York: Anchor, 1995.

Luey, Beth, ed. *Revising Your Dissertation: Advice from Leading Editors*. Revised edition. Berkeley: University of California Press, 2008.

Mackey, Nathaniel. "The Art of Poetry No. 107." Interview with Cathy Park Hong. *Paris Review*, no. 232 (Spring 2020). https://www.theparisreview.org/interviews/7534/the-art-of-poetry-no-107-nathaniel-mackey

McPhee, John. *Draft No. 4: On the Writing Process*. New York: Farrar, Straus and Giroux, 2017.

Morrison, Toni. "The Art of Fiction No. 134." Interview with Elissa Chappell and Claudia Brodsky Lacour. *Paris Review*, no. 128 (Fall 1993). https://www.theparisreview.org/interviews/1888/the-art-of-fiction-no-134-toni-morrison

Online Writing Lab, Purdue University. owl.purdue.edu

Sewell, David. "It's for Sale, So It Must Be Finished: Digital Projects in the Scholarly Publishing World." *Digital Humanities Quarterly* 3, no. 2 (2009).

Shiller, Robert. *Narrative Economics: How Stories Go Viral and Drive Major Economic Change.* Princeton, NJ: Princeton University Press, 2019.

Silverman, Kaja. *The Miracle of Analogy, or The History of Photography, Part 1.* Stanford: Stanford University Press, 2015.

Steiner, George. *On Difficulty and Other Essays.* Oxford: Oxford University Press, 1980.

Strunk, William, Jr., and E. B. White, *The Elements of Style,* 4th ed. London: Pearson, 1999.

Sword, Helen. *Stylish Academic Writing.* Cambridge, MA: Harvard University Press, 2012.

Warner, John. *Why They Can't Write: Killing the Five-Paragraph Essay and Other Necessities.* Baltimore: Johns Hopkins University Press, 2018.

Index